"Vivian Fransen has written an
well-told love stories, the reader
find our footing when her perfec
and throughout her journey to w
human resiliency is perhaps the most divine thing about us."
—Carolyn S. Briggs, author of *Higher Ground: A Memoir of
Salvation Found and Lost*

"The struggles between a gay husband and a straight spouse
are so painful because, in most cases, the love between the two
partners still exists. This memoir is written from the heart, is
honest, shows empathy, and ultimately provides hope, which
is something every straight spouse desperately needs."
—Francine Barbetta, PsyD, author of *A Pebble In His Shoe:
The Diary Of A Straight Spouse*, website: drbarbetta.com

"Vivian Fransen's honest and touching memoir of her process
in experiencing her spouse's coming out as a gay man
demonstrates levels of insight that can be immeasurably
helpful to anyone in a similar situation. Her chronicle
leads the reader from an alcohol-influenced disclosure through
the pain and confusion of disentangling from love and an
unpromising relationship. Vivian writes this with an emotional
intelligence infused with growing clarity and compassion for
her husband and herself. It will be my go-to recommendation
for those experiencing such a challenging life experience."
—Chuck Rhoades, PhD

"With vivid and lively prose, Vivian Fransen has written an
honest memoir of her marriage with all its love, complexity,
and surprising turns. As her husband begins to come to grips
with being gay, Fransen takes the reader on the difficult
journey of the straight spouse. As a pastor, I know this book
will be useful to clergy in helping Christian couples facing this
complicated reality and to straight spouses who want to know
they can find help and hope."
—Rev. Cynthia Cochran-Carney, Presbyterian pastor

"In a no-holds-barred memoir, Vivian Fransen details the ways her world is rocked when her husband discloses that he might be gay. She expresses emotions ranging from shock and fear to self-doubt, vulnerability, anger, resignation, determination, and humor as she journeys toward new love and reconnection with her Christian faith."
—Melanie Davis, PhD, author of *Look Within: A Woman's Journal*, website: melaniedavisphd.com

"This is a must-read for anyone experiencing the shock of a partner coming out as gay. Ms. Fransen's very personal story is filled with her pain, her questioning of her own worth, her survival, and her eventual growth and triumph. It is inspirational and heartwarming, yet a reality that is not uncommon in our fast-changing society."
—Constance M. Bowes, PhD, human sexuality therapist, conniebowes@gmail.com

The Straight Spouse: A Memoir

By Vivian Fransen

Open Door Publications

The Straight Spouse: A Memoir
By Vivian Fransen

Published by
Open Door Publications
2113 Stackhouse Dr.
Yardley, PA 19067
www.OpenDoorPublications.com

To my nieces, nephews, and godchildren
when they ask,
"What really happened to Aunt Vee Vee back then?"
and my therapist, "Dr. Barley,"
with never-ending gratitude for being my lifeline
throughout my journey of despair
and putting Humpty Dumpty back together again
with a renewed zest for living life to its fullest

"Dare to declare who you are. It is not far from the shores of silence to the boundaries of speech. The path is not long, but the way is deep. You must not only walk there, you must be prepared to leap."

—Author Unknown (often erroneously attributed to Hildegard of Bingen [1098-1179])

Preface

"Let me in," you say, as if a simple flick of the wrist will release the deadbolt lock so I can swing the door wide open.

No, in my case, the door is monstrously heavy, built to be impenetrable and now so warped, with hinges rusted and seized over time, I can barely budge it. Do you have a crowbar? Perhaps you can push while I pull with all my might. Or maybe there's another way. Is there a window to crawl through?

Oh, you want to be in the same room as my feelings? That room is in the darkest, most unkempt, and rundown corner of the house, full of cobwebs, broken furniture, and rancid odors. Keep out. Danger zone: Wear hard hats at all times. You see, with me it's all about mind over feelings. Minimize feelings at all cost; they only get in the way. You know, not every woman is a gushing fountain of emotions.

Let's go in anyhow? If you insist. And only because I somehow trust you not to declare me a hopeless mess.

Chapter 1

My marriage began to fall apart in the wee hours of the morning after St. Patrick's Day 1990.

Neither Irish nor Catholic, Victor Locatelli—my husband of nearly 12 years—and I had embraced the spirit of the holiday earlier that night as a childfree couple in our 30s. We wore shamrock green shirts with comfortable jeans and made sure we had a hearty stock of wine and hard liquor in the house.

"It feels great to have a weekend at home without any job or social commitments," said Victor, pouring a third glass of Merlot for me and a chaser of Jack Daniel's for himself. "No stress and no hassles."

I agreed. I wanted to unwind, relax, and have fun together. I had a million things on my mind and was trying to shake off the uneasy feeling I had about our disturbing conversation two days earlier.

"Remember last year when we decided to hang out with my friends from work at the Irish pub?" I asked, sitting down on my side of the loveseat next to our terrier mutt, Champ—a Toto lookalike from *The Wizard of Oz* movie. "No more corned beef and cabbage served with those never-ending mugs of green beer. I like staying in, safe and sound, without worrying about drunk drivers."

"And now that I finally quit smoking, I don't want to be around all those bar crawlers smoking their brains out," he said, fidgeting with his shot glass as if silently calculating how to pace his drinking to maximize the buzz.

Victor stepped over to the stereo, watched the arm of the automatic record changer swing back to release the next album from the stack of LPs on the turntable, and then cranked up the volume of the Robert Cray album he had recently bought. He sang along with the lyrics of "The Forecast Calls for Pain" as he settled himself into the high-back easy chair facing the log burning in the fireplace.

"Man, that's great songwriting," he said. "It makes me want to grab my guitar and write a new song of my own."

"Ah, I love to hear you play, especially all those love songs you composed about me," I said, longing to recapture the early days in our relationship when we were going to college together in New England during the mid-1970s.

~~~

Our relationship was so fluid and easy way back then, grooving to the music of John Denver's *Windsong* and Carole King's *Tapestry*. Victor and I struck up a friendship early in our sophomore year at a Bible college when I was making adjustments in my social life. Allison, my roommate and best friend, had recently abandoned her education as a music major because of her personal tug-of-war between developing her singing voice and smoking cigarettes. Instead of returning to college, she decided to live at home with her parents and take an entry-level job at an insurance company. Allison was also the "first serious girlfriend" of lovestruck Victor, who was trying to pick up the pieces after she dumped him over the summer. She told me she broke up with him because she preferred a taller boyfriend as a dance partner so she could wear shoes with higher heels.

During our first year of college, I sometimes tagged along when Allison and Victor were together—crossing the street at all hours to be off campus "for smokes" (even though I was a nonsmoker) or studying for a test or playing cards or singing Jesus songs together with our commuter student friend Marty, who lived in an apartment with his wife and baby daughter. Allison was a statuesque woman with long black hair and a keen sense of fashion. (Picture a size 12 version of Marlo Thomas in the 1960s TV sitcom *That Girl*—with more curves and cleavage.) She had a sort of edgy attitude about life and was often the object of male attention.

At the risk of being expelled from college, Allison and I sometimes drank rum-and-Diet-Pepsi concoctions in our dorm room and took excursions to a local nightclub for whiskey sours. I was a bookworm and wallflower with fantasies of someday undergoing an ugly-duckling-to-swan metamorphosis, clueless about developing an attractive appearance and consoling myself with such mantras as "I prefer to nurture my inner beauty." Adopting the librarian look with my Peter Pan–collared blouses, smock-style clothes, and practical Mary Jane shoes, I admired Allison for her sophistication and how Victor went out of his way to cater to her in every way he could.

Our shared loss of Allison provided common ground for bonding when Victor and I returned to college in September 1975. As our friendship grew stronger, we flirted with the notion of becoming a couple. After our first awkward kiss in the dark at Cana Pond, we started to fall in love.

Victor had thick brown hair, expressive brown eyes, a clear complexion, and an infectious laugh, along with a boyish rascal look. His features reminded me of Dustin Hoffman in *The Graduate*—quite a package for me and my country girl from Vermont ways.

Victor was my first and only boyfriend; I was incredulous with the notion that somebody could actually love me. I was anticipating a life as a spinster; I didn't think I would ever find a man who would love me unconditionally, "just as I am." Every day I praised God for Victor, a marvelous gift from a loving God.

Much to my dismay, Allison and I drifted apart when she discovered I was romantically involved with Victor. Even though she had put him in her discard pile, it was too unsettling knowing we were intimate with the same guy. (I had never heard the popular wisdom, "Thou shalt not date thy roommate's ex-boyfriend"—something that doesn't show up in the student orientation manual at a Bible college.)

Victor and I spent every moment we possibly could together, inextricably linked, walking hand in hand, from our first morning class—eating meals together, working as Food Service employees in the cafeteria together, attending or skipping chapel together, studying together—until midnight curfew when we returned to our separate sleeping quarters. We shared our deepest secrets and wildest dreams. Finding solace in sharing insights about our experiences growing up in dysfunctional families, we spent hours discussing self-help books, such as *I'm OK—You're OK* by Thomas Harris, MD, and *How to Be Your Own Best Friend* by Mildred Newman, Bernard Berkowitz, and Jean Owen.

We were soul mates. We read the Bible together and prayed together. We enjoyed an active sex life (no intercourse until we became engaged because we believed that was God's plan for our lives) and were discreet enough to avoid the embarrassment and negative consequences of being caught by college authorities. A muscular, rock-solid man with a magnetic personality, Victor made me feel like the most cherished woman on the planet with his adoring eyes and masterful lovemaking.

After saving our money from summer employment and various part-time jobs while attending college, we planned, orchestrated, and paid for every detail of our wedding, which we held two weeks after we graduated. We exchanged our vows at a seaside church, reciting our carefully chosen words from memory without any prompts from the young minister who officiated our wedding. Inspired by Art Garfunkel's recording of "I Only Have Eyes for You," we claimed it as our love song. We stared with dreamy eyes at each other during our first dance as bride and groom at our wedding reception held in a fancy hotel. Victor wrote our wedding song, which was performed as part of our wedding ceremony by our good friend Marty, who played the guitar and sang these lyrics:

Lord, we come in your presence
Two lovers for you to behold
Bowing down, Lord, please hear our prayer
That we would cherish and care forevermore
That we would cherish and care forevermore

~~~

"Hey, there," said Victor, rising up from across the room and making his best effort to sound like David Bowie. "Ground Control to Major Tom. You ready for another glass of wine?"

"No, thanks. I'm still working on this one."

"Oh, come on," he teased, as he poured himself a tall glass of Jack Daniel's and added some ice cubes from the freezer. "You're no fun. You're not going to let me drink alone, are you?"

"Okay, bring it on. Let's drink the night away."

As I held my glass of wine by the bowl, not the stem, for a greater sense of security to avoid any spills, I gazed up at the wood beams supporting the cathedral ceiling of our family room. This was our favorite space in the seven-room townhome we had recently purchased (with a generous loan from Victor's parents to help with the down payment) in Somerset County, New Jersey, after living in rentals our entire married life.

Listening to Sting sing "If You Love Somebody, Set Them Free," I had an odd feeling about the lyrics, something I could no longer ignore. Did Victor feel trapped these days? I found myself reconstructing the conversation Victor had started two days earlier. Cold sober, he had asked me how I would feel about having an open marriage. He insisted our marriage was strong enough to handle such an arrangement, and he wanted me to be open to the possibility should his "self-growth" warrant it.

I had felt a stab of hurt feelings but quickly dismissed them, and then silently questioned myself: Did I do something wrong? Was I not paying enough attention to him? Was he looking for more excitement in our sex life? Why would he even consider an open marriage?

"Absolutely not!" I had declared. "Are you crazy? Infidelity is a betrayal of our marriage vows. No way! Is this your way of telling me you aren't happy in our marriage anymore?"

"No, that's not what I'm saying. Never mind. Forget I ever mentioned it."

"Are you seeing someone else?"

"No, there isn't any 'someone else,'" said Victor in a sad voice. "I was just thinking. But I see you're not gonna budge on this. So never mind. End of conversation."

Then he had stormed out of the room and retreated to spend the evening upstairs in what we call our Things-To-Do room—a place full of yet-to-be-read books and magazines, musical instruments, games, hobbies, and a desk for sorting through the mail, paying the bills, and handling all our household paperwork. I dutifully dropped the subject, preferring to pretend his words were some sort of temporary insanity that would simply disappear.

But that conversation two days earlier was still on my mind. Strains from Fine Young Cannibals blasting "She Drives Me Crazy" from the stereo shook me out of my reverie. Victor looked quite intoxicated, slumped down in his chair, and I was inebriated, too. I took Champ outside the back door to pee and returned to the loveseat, poised for confrontation.

"You know, I've been thinking about all this talk about open marriage," I said, twirling a clump of my shoulder-length blonde hair with my index finger. "We need to talk about what's going on with you. I need you to be totally honest with me."

"Oh, come on. Let's not go there tonight. We're having a party."

"But I really need to know," I said, feeling empowered in my wine-fueled state. "If you're not happy with me anymore, we need to talk about it."

"Trust me. You really don't want to know what's going on with me," he mumbled.

"Of course I do. You are the love of my life!"

"Like I said, you really don't want to know."

"Stop saying that," I said, making direct eye contact with him. "I'll keep nagging you about this so come clean now. You ask me about having an open marriage and then drop the subject? I'm not stupid. Something's going on, and you need to tell me."

Paul Simon's "50 Ways to Leave Your Lover" started playing on the stereo.

"By the way, under the circumstances, this is not my idea of party music," I said, standing up to turn down the volume.

"You are so sensitive, Vivian. You're always reading way more meaning into every word. You're always analyzing every detail. You just don't know how to let things go."

"Let things go? We're talking about our marriage, the only real constant in our lives. Nothing could be more important to me than you."

"We all make sacrifices in life. As Mick Jagger sings, 'you can't always get what you want' and all that."

"What can that possibly mean? You think fidelity's a sacrifice? That's ridiculous. I don't know what's happened to you, Victor. Have you lost your mind? And enough already with all the song lyrics."

"The truth is that I still haven't found what I'm looking for."

I paused, feeling uncertain, confused, and afraid about what else Victor had to say. "What do you mean? You found me! You have someone who loves you to pieces, no matter what, forever and ever, amen."

"You aren't the problem," said Victor. "I'm the problem."

"So tell me about it," I said, leaning in toward him. "Have you met someone special at work?" That's all I could figure out because we were always together except when we were both at work.

"I already told you," he said, taking a swig of his drink. "I'm not seeing anyone. I don't have any extracurricular activities."

"It must be another woman. You have to tell me. I need to know."

"Listen to me," he spoke slowly and slurred his words. "You never, ever, have to worry about me being with another woman. That will never happen. What you do have to worry about is me being with another man."

I stared at him, stunned and unable to accept the gravity of his words. The music stopped. I sat still, barely breathing. Was this some sort of cruel joke? It was too outrageous to be true.

"A man, not another woman?" It seemed impossible that my Italian stud husband could even think about having sex with a man. "No problem, I'll just go for a sex change operation," I joked.

"I'm serious. And I can't believe I just told you this. I must be really drunk."

I watched as he staggered out of his chair and stumbled up the stairs, too wasted to do anything except pass out on the bed.

Chapter 2

After I threw up several times in the downstairs bathroom, I climbed the stairs and headed for the Things-To-Do room, with Champ following close behind. I fell in a heap on the stained carpet in the corner of the room and then sat cross-legged, rocking back and forth. Champ cocked her head to the side, looking puzzled by my unusual behavior.

How could this be, I wondered. I never saw this coming. I'd never even heard of this sort of thing happening to a happily married couple. *Wait*, I told myself, *I had to stop thinking of us as a happily married couple.*

My mind went into analytical overdrive. How in the world could I help my husband with this issue? I didn't have a clue where to begin. I certainly didn't have any books on married couples who start questioning their sexual orientation. Were there any such books? Doesn't anyone with such questions wrestle with them long before turning 30 years old? Who in their right mind would marry before resolving such a critical issue as their sexual orientation? Can people change their sexual orientation over time?

What was I supposed to do—somehow grow a penis to make my husband happy? I needed to fix this problem. I tried to think this out on my own. I could come up with tons of questions, but no answers.

What did this say about me as a woman? I guessed it meant that living with Vivian for 12 years can make a man go gay. But that's crazy. How could that be possible? I don't have that kind of power. What on earth did I do or didn't do to bring this on? What a total idiot I must be to let this happen. I never even knew I was supposed to worry about this sort of thing.

I wondered what would happen to me next. My situation seemed hopeless, and I felt so lost and alone. So I retreated to that dark place within myself, flooded with a profound sense of doom. The more I thought about how incapable I was of handling this severe blow, the greater the temptation to remove myself permanently. *This may be a good time for me to die*, I thought. I'd already had a full life, even with a few setbacks along the way. My no-win situation was unbearable, a dead end. This was not self-pity; this was the smart thing to do. It was better to check out than endure the pain of this rejection.

"Self-destruct over a man? I thought Vivian had more sense than that!" That's what people would say. But they wouldn't understand how dead I felt inside.

And where was God in all this? How could a loving God—the same God that brought Victor and me together—possibly allow me to be in this predicament? Even Job—who suffered the tragic loss of his health, his family, and his wealth—didn't have to contend with a spouse with same-gender feelings, as far as I knew. Or was there a footnote in the Bible I somehow missed?

I was too overwhelmed to search for a greater purpose in all this; the only Bible verse that came to mind was "there shall be wailing and gnashing of teeth." Weeping was the only thing I could manage to do. The tears just wouldn't stop coming no matter how I tried to gain some degree of control. Even Champ slinked away, with her tail low to the floor, to curl up in a ball and sleep in the master bedroom with Victor.

~~~

Drowning in the chaos of my jumbled thoughts, I realized I needed solid ground. So I took a mental inventory of my relationship with Victor and traced our evolution as a couple: our college days, our intense desire to be with one another, all those love letters, our field service together as crisis intervention counselors, our wedding, our honeymoon on Cape Cod and Nantucket, our road trip out West, our work as houseparents in Oregon that first year of marriage, our return back East, our career struggles, dealing with the demands of our families, our dream vacation in Europe, and finally the joy of being proud homeowners with meaningful jobs and relative financial security. We always scraped each other off the floor when hard times bulldozed through and were steadfast in encouraging one another to be the best we could be—every step of the way.

I scoured my memory for any clues to suggest Victor was sexually attracted to men, but came up with nothing.

I pondered the many hundreds of times—could it be thousands?—we made love, sometimes adventurous, sometimes conventional, including all the times we had pure, sweat-drenched, mind-blowing sex. We had intimate knowledge of every inch of each other's body. Yet, I couldn't identify anything, even remotely, gay about him.

Was I so blinded by my love for Victor and my desperate need to be loved that I couldn't see clearly? Had he been living a lie all those years? From that moment on, everything about our life together became suspect.

~~~

As dawn approached, I watched the morning light and continued to stare off into space, wide awake and too distraught to sleep. Within a few hours, Victor stuck his head in the room.

"Are you still awake from last night?"

"Yes," I whimpered. "And I need to warn you: I'm an absolute train wreck."

"Oh no. I was afraid you might take this hard. Let me hold you."

I stood up and walked over to the doorway. He wrapped his strong arms around me as I cried.

"I can't seem to pull myself together. It feels like something died. I can't stop crying. I can't think straight—oh, I guess that's the wrong word to say now."

"Oh," Victor cooed. "You're taking this so hard."

"What am I supposed to do? I don't have a clue what to do."

"Listen, I'm so sorry I opened my big mouth last night. I don't know what got into me. I think it's the Prozac. It seems to work like a truth serum on me."

I felt too scattered at that moment to deal with his apology and rehash what he had told me last night.

"I've never felt so low," I said. "Maybe I'm having some sort of mental breakdown. I'm such a basket case."

"Vivian, look at me. You are a beautiful woman. I still love you. I'm not going anywhere. I will never leave you nor forsake you."

"What? How can you say that? Our world has fallen apart. More specifically, our marriage has fallen apart. It's over."

"No, it's not. We're still together. Let's see what happens."

I couldn't understand how Victor could be so at ease the morning following his earthshaking revelation. I felt we were doomed, as if the sure-footed path ahead for our marriage had become a treacherous field of land mines. It seemed clear he had needs I couldn't possibly fulfill. Giving him all my love didn't matter anymore; I didn't have what it takes to make him happy.

"How can you act so calm, Victor? My life is shattered."

"It's not the end of the world. Slow down and take a few deep breaths."

I backed away from him and leaned against the door.

"Okay, let me take a shower and put on some clean clothes. Maybe that will help me get a grip on today. Thank God it's Sunday. Oh, no, I can't even think about how I'm ever going to pull myself together for work tomorrow or beyond."

"One step at a time. I'll make some coffee and take care of Champ while you get ready. We have all day together. We'll make the best of it."

12

~~~

When I came downstairs after my shower, Victor was reading *The New York Times*. He stood up, pulled out the kitchen chair for me, and poured me a cup of black coffee.

"Do you feel better now?" he asked.

"I feel washed up, but I'm so wiped out," I said, as I broke into tears. "I had no idea I could cry so much."

"Listen, I've got an idea. Let's take a ride to Flemington. We'll look around and do some shopping. It'll be good for us to get out of the house."

I agreed it made sense to do something else so I wouldn't stay home and wallow in my tears all day. I needed to gain some perspective. Perhaps a ride in the country would help.

"We can try, but I may embarrass you in public with all this sobbing," I said.

"I don't care about what strangers think. Let's go now."

~~~

Leaving Champ behind at home, we locked up the house, climbed in our blue Toyota Celica, and made our way to Flemington—a mecca for outlet shopping. While Victor flipped through the car radio dial to find some upbeat tunes, I stared out the window; the fields and hills looked cold and lifeless to me. After we parked near the hub of the main shops, we meandered around the shoe store, some jewelry stores, and the coat factory. I was teary but silent as Victor herded me through the crowds. Holding my hand, he led me to a lingerie store and motioned for me to step inside.

"Lingerie? Are you kidding?" I said, feeling awkward and confused. "Is this for me or for you?"

"Very funny," said Victor, with a sarcastic smirk. "No, it's for you. Let's see what they have."

"But you know I'm a flannel-nightgown-and-knee-socks kind of woman. That's the way we like it: bare skin and accessible genitals—that's all we ever needed to start our engines. Or has that changed now?"

"Not at all," he said, scanning the racks of intimate apparel.

"I don't have to put on slinky, lacy underthings to feel sexy. In fact, foreplay is all about taking off our clothes, not putting any on."

"I know, but I want you to go through this store and choose anything you like and as much as you like. Here, what about this outfit?"

I looked at the skimpy, baby doll nightie with pink lace he held up.

"I don't think so. That would barely cover me. And take a look at this price tag—"

"Oh, come on," he said. "I want you to pick out some pretty things for yourself."

"I appreciate the thought, but this isn't necessary. Besides, you know if Champ gets ahold of this underwear, she'll tear it to shreds." The dog already had a fetish for underpants left in the dirty clothes basket.

Several hundred dollars later—with tears streaming down my face from yet another crying jag, my nose running a steady flow, and my energy too spent to put up any resistance in the checkout line—we left the store with a ton of lingerie.

~~~

When we arrived home, Victor suggested I try on some of the new purchases. I vetoed the idea, claiming my face, feeling as if it had a bad case of diaper rash, would clearly kill the mood. I later stuffed the bags of lingerie in the back of the linen closet and quickly dismissed their existence.

Victor decided it was time for some "comfort food." He filled a large pasta pot with water and suggested I chop some vegetables for a salad. We worked side by side in preparing dinner. When everything was ready, we sat down at the kitchen table together.

Victor ate a hearty meal while I pushed the food around my plate with a fork and fed table scraps to Champ.

"Is there any chance what you said last night was an early April Fools' Day joke in very bad taste?"

"Ah, no, that's not the case," he said as he chewed his food.

"I didn't think so, but I was hoping. You do have a reputation for playing practical jokes on people. Remember during our college days how you and Marty would troll the streets in his wreck of a car in the middle of the winter and roll down your window at traffic lights and say, 'Pardon me, would you have any Grey Poupon?'"

"But of course," said Victor with a fake British accent.

We both laughed.

"Most people would giggle, but not everyone was amused. You really get off on the shock value of saying the unexpected."

"And you remember the first words I ever said to you?" Victor asked.

"Well, yes I do. That's another example of how you enjoy creating a scene."

I recalled the first time I met Victor. He had come up to me with a tray full of food in the college cafeteria and sat down at the table where Allison and I were eating with a bunch of other students. People were sharing their latest spiritual insights from reading the Bible during their early morning devotions.

Then Victor injected himself into the conversation by staring at me and saying, "Hi, I'm Victor. When was the first day of your last menstrual period?"

I burst out laughing because his question was a refreshing departure from the Bible-quoting conversations of the self-righteous students at the table. Without missing a beat, I answered his question, not caring a bit about revealing such private data about myself. I thought Victor had a clever way of making his point: Perhaps a person's daily devotions were something personal and private, like a woman's menstrual cycle, not to be the routine focus for public discourse. The others at the table immediately stood up and left the table in disgust, leaving the three of us—Allison, Victor, and me—alone to talk.

"I was a bit of a clown, or I guess you could call me a jerk, back then," said Victor. "I'm glad to say I never really fit in with some of those Bible majors. Remember how some of those guys would go through magazines, cutting out all the pictures of beautiful women in ads and throwing them away, to keep themselves and 'other brethren' from the temptation of using them as masturbation visuals? On the other hand, some of the jocks in my dorm would get a kick out of urinating on other guys as a joke. I got a lot of mixed messages there."

"Speaking about mixed messages, let's talk about you. How long have you been struggling with these same-gender feelings?"

"I can't really say."

"Have you talked to anyone about this?"

"Not really," said Victor, leaning down to scratch Champ's head. "When I had my physical, I told the doctor I had recently quit smoking and was feeling depressed. I also mentioned I have trouble falling asleep. When he asked me what I think about when I can't fall asleep, I told the truth: I think about being with a man. He ignored my response, but gave me a prescription for Prozac to help with the depression and sent me on my way."

"So what are you going to do about these feelings?"

"I don't know. I honestly don't know."

"Have you already acted on these feelings?"

"So many questions," said Victor with a sigh. "Is this some sort of interrogation?"

"I just want to talk this through."

"Well, I am who I am. I don't know what to say. I can tell you I have daily torture about these feelings. The feelings are so strong."

"Daily torture? You are suffering every day about this?"

16

I ached inside for him, trying to imagine for a moment these alien yearnings.

"So maybe that's why you drink so much—"

"I don't have a drinking problem," he said, as he pounded his fist on the table. "And I never miss a day of work. So don't start. And don't try to be my therapist. Never ask questions that will lead to answers you aren't prepared to handle. That's what we learned as crisis intervention counselors in college."

"But what good is all that training when the crisis is happening to us? You're right. I certainly am not prepared to handle anything you say about this. I need a plan. I need a plan for me."

"Well, now that I let the genie out of the bottle, I guess there's no turning back," he said.

"I don't know what you're going to do. But I need help. I desperately need help."

I told him I would go to work the next day and ask my friend Connie in Human Resources to give me the name of a good therapist. I'd say I need help with a family problem, making it clear it wasn't a work problem. And if I couldn't see someone right away, I'd call our minister.

"Victor, do I have your permission to speak candidly to Pastor Norman about all this? You know he's obligated to keep everything confidential."

"Of course, you can talk to Norman."

"I know you two are friends," I said. Victor and Norman had gone out for a few beers together. "Does he know anything about this?"

"No, we've never discussed my same-gender feelings. I like Norman, but not in any way you would find objectionable."

"Okay, that's my plan."

"Good idea," he said, as he reached over for my hand and clasped it in his. "We'll get through all this. Somehow."

~~~

17

Later that night, we crawled into bed, exhausted from the emotions of the day. I wanted to believe Victor's motivation for the spontaneous lingerie shopping spree was to affirm my femininity as a sexually desirable woman. Or perhaps spending money on me was his way of showing remorse. Or, I wondered, could it be the start of some sort of cross-dressing fetish Victor wanted to explore?

I felt exhausted by all the mind racing and confusion and emotional chaos. I needed to switch to autopilot. My brain was fried, overwhelmed without any sleep for the past 36 hours. All I knew for sure was I still loved Victor, unconditionally, no matter what.

In our brass bed together naked, under our blankets in the dark, we made skin-to-skin contact. Then, somehow, a spark of passion ignited. We instinctively grasped for the familiar, craving the intimacy that was at risk, letting our bodies communicate through touch without any words getting in the way.

Chapter 3

The next morning Victor and I commenced our morning "hurry-up-and-get-ready-and-don't-be-late-for-work" routines, ever grateful for the luxury of two bathrooms. With a kiss at the door, we headed off in separate cars for our daily commute—as if that day were no different than any other Monday.

Dressed in a suit and tie, Victor dashed off to his job as a computer programmer in a telecommunications company. He had recently changed careers, after working as a counselor in a county youth shelter, managing a group home for adults with severe developmental disabilities, running a surgical supply store, and then graduating from a computer programming training institute. He did outstanding work.

I was at the peak of my young career as a communications officer at a grantmaking foundation—a dream come true. I had worked as a hospital grants administrator, a university development officer, an assistant administrator in a hospice program, and a healthcare worker in a family planning clinic. After earning a master's degree in public administration, I made it my personal goal to someday work in the foundation world. I considered myself the world's luckiest woman to land this job six months earlier and become part of the Foundation's "family."

But my mission that day was to find a crackerjack therapist, someone to help me navigate this crisis in my marriage. When I arrived at work, I made a beeline to Connie in Human Resources and asked her for a recommendation. She gave me contact information for a psychologist, Dr. Barley. I closed the door to my office and made the telephone call. His receptionist scheduled me for my first appointment—10 days away, which seemed an eternity to me. Then I made another telephone call.

"Pastor Norman, I'm in trouble and need some prayer. Is there any way I can meet with you today?"

"Does four o'clock work for you?"

"Perfect! I can't thank you enough."

~~~

I left my workplace early and drove to his office, which was located in the back of the Presbyterian Church. I took a deep breath and found my way to his study. Pastor Norman, a 30-something man with a neatly trimmed beard and wearing jeans and a sweater, responded to my knock and greeted me at the door.

"Vivian, come on in."

"I really appreciate you seeing me on such short notice," I said as I sat down in the wooden chair in front of his desk. "I need some sort of spiritual Band-Aid for the personal crisis that popped up out of nowhere over the weekend. I'm smart enough to know I need some professional help with a therapist, but the soonest appointment I could arrange is for next week. So here I am with you."

"I'm glad you're here. What's going on?"

"My husband dropped a bomb on me."

I then gave him the rundown on Victor's confession.

~~~

"I don't have a clue what to do to help my husband," I said, clutching the arms of the chair. "This isn't supposed to happen to us. Victor is the man of my dreams. He professes to be a committed, born-again Christian. He's made marriage vows to me that include '...leaving all others, I will keep myself for you alone.' Now he decides he's not 100 percent heterosexual? How can this happen?"

"Oh my, Vivian," said Pastor Norman. "No wonder you're so upset. This is quite a shock."

"And before you ask, let me just say our sex life has never been a problem, as far as I know. We've always been sexually compatible. God knows, we spent most of our college days with our hands down each other's pants. We're healthy, fun-loving, sexual beings, the way God made us. Victor is the only boyfriend I've ever had; if it wasn't for him, I wouldn't even know what romantic love is."

"What does Victor say about all this?"

"He says he can't believe he told me. He blames his Prozac for acting as a truth serum. He says he never intended to tell me about his same-gender feelings because he doesn't want to hurt me. He also says he doesn't know what to do about it now. Neither do I."

I grabbed a tissue and wiped the tears falling down my cheeks.

"Is there anything in the Bible that speaks to this?" I said.

"I can't find any verse in Scripture about what to do when your husband turns gay. Never in a million years did I think this would happen to us."

"To be perfectly honest, my training at seminary didn't prepare me for anything like this. I think you're doing the right thing to seek help from a professional therapist with experience in this area."

"Oh, I see," my far-fetched hope for a quick spiritual fix deflated.

Was I in the middle of something too complicated for clergy guidance? It hadn't occurred to me that reaching out to my minister might lead to a dead end. Did I have unrealistic expectations, believing God would use him to help me find some spiritual meaning in the midst of this crisis? Still, I found some comfort in telling someone I could trust about my situation. I gave Pastor Norman credit for showing compassion toward me and not trying to gloss over my predicament with well-meaning platitudes.

"I really appreciate your honesty and your confidentiality. I assured Victor you wouldn't post any notices in the church bulletin requesting prayers for his same-gender feelings."

21

He smiled at me. I could tell he was amused by my attempt to lighten the mood with some humor.

"You're right about that. This is a private matter that doesn't leave this office without your permission. So what can I do for you?"

"A word of prayer would be most helpful. I don't even know how to pray about this—I thought we were already living God's plan for our lives."

"Let's pray now."

As we bowed our heads, I closed my eyes as tight as I could.

"Our Heavenly Father, we come to you today, full of pain and uncertainty about the future for Victor and Vivian. We ask for your guidance and wisdom. We ask for peace in the midst of anxiety. We know you are a loving and almighty God who works in our lives for good purposes. Thank you for your presence now and during the coming days. Remind Vivian in so many ways that nothing can separate her from your love as Lord of her life. In Jesus' name, Amen."

"Amen," I echoed.

I left his office, with a yearning for a protective covering for my exposed state—like a larva in dire need of spinning its own cocoon.

~~~

When I arrived home, Victor was already there, opening a can of Mighty Dog for Champ in the kitchen.

"How did everything go?" he asked.

"Good." I placed my briefcase on a kitchen chair and took my coat off. "I made an appointment with a therapist for next week and met with Pastor Norman just now. He's concerned about both of us."

I then reconstructed our conversation.

Victor listened without interruption and gazed at me, as if he were surveying the damage to a cherished landmark after a storm.

"I know this is really hard for you," he said. "It's hard for me, too. It feels like we're in uncharted territory. We're sort of up a creek without a paddle."

"Yeah, without a map and without a compass. Strong winds are blowing us away, and we're in danger of capsizing. And I'm the one who can't swim."

"But you're grabbing for a life jacket. So you can float if the boat sinks. And I'm right beside you, kicking and thrashing through the water."

"Okay, now I'm feeling seasick."

We both laughed when we realized we were getting carried away with all the nautical metaphors.

"Actually, I'm thinking we should go upstairs, take off our clothes, and go to bed. I want to make love to you, Vivian."

"Now? Before supper?"

"Yes. Let's do it. Now."

So we did.

Chapter 4

"Don't you think it's a bit strange we're behaving like sex maniacs in the midst of a cataclysmic rupture in our marriage?" I asked Victor at breakfast after nine days of carrying on with our lives as if nothing had changed.

"Perhaps. But it's the best way I know to reassure you about us."

"You mean we're using sex as our security blanket?"

"Something like that."

"Well, whatever happens, we certainly know the issue isn't low libido," I said, noting the countdown of days for my long-awaited visit with a therapist had finally come on this day.

~~~

Somewhat apprehensive, I found Dr. Barley's office and arrived 15 minutes early to fill out paperwork, as instructed by the receptionist. I responded to each item on the intake questionnaire, hoping my case would be interesting enough for this highly respected therapist to accept me in his caseload. I had no energy to shop around for another therapist.

Dr. Barley—a tall, well-groomed man wearing a dark suit, with an athletic look and welcoming smile—escorted me to his inner office and immediately put me at ease. At the end of the 90-minute session, he asked if I would like to meet with him again. I accepted his offer, which became the beginning of weekly therapy sessions for several years to come.

~~~

Later that day when I came home, Victor met me at the front door with a kiss and wanted to know all about it.

"It went well. I think you'd like him, too. Very professional. He listens carefully to everything I say. And he seems more interested in me than what's going on with you. I feel as if I'm the center of his attention."

"Of course you are. You're the client. He's the therapist. That's his job: to help you."

"Well, he did say a few things I need to make perfectly clear with you about boundaries. He said my health and safety come first. He recommends we both get tested for any sexually transmitted infections."

"Why is that necessary?"

"I told him you haven't acted on your same-gender feelings, but he insists we both have a checkup with different doctors about our sex-related health."

"I can do that," said Victor. "I have nothing to hide. As I've told you, I haven't done anything wrong."

I felt reassured that Victor was willing to comply with Dr. Barley's advice without any resistance. I believed Victor when he said he was not messing around with someone else. He was the one who spilled the truth about his daily torment; I didn't doubt his fidelity. He had never lied to me before, as far as I knew.

"Also, we need to agree to be totally honest about any sexual contact with anyone else that occurs as soon as it happens," I said. "It's a matter of personal integrity, as well as a matter of life and death."

"That sounds rather melodramatic."

"Dr. Barley said we're not allowed to waste time and energy guessing or suspecting or lying or playing detective. It's your responsibility to tell me the truth, and it's my responsibility to accept the truth. Regardless of what else happens, no sexual contact between us if there's any sexual contact with anyone else. Period. Are you willing to do this?"

"Of course. That makes sense. You know, that's a real issue for me. Here we are, smack in the middle of the AIDS epidemic. Bummer timing, to say the least."

I agreed. I was well aware AIDS was a death sentence in 1990, with nearly twice as many Americans dead due to AIDS as those who had died in the Vietnam War.

"Okay, if that's settled, we can move forward," I said. "It's clear my emotional dependence on you isn't healthy for either of us."

I had told Dr. Barley that Victor and I have a sort of Krazy Glue bond with one another—extremely strong and nearly impossible to pull apart. I was determined to do whatever was required to make our marriage work. I saw Victor's responsiveness to my description of my first therapy session as a good sign: I felt we were on the same side in facing this challenge in our marriage.

"I'm proud of you for having the courage to see a therapist," said Victor. "Does Dr. Barley want to meet me?"

"That hasn't come up yet. But he did invite me to meet with him again next week. And you know what else? I was bold enough to ask him if he's married. I know therapists don't usually reveal anything about their personal life. But he said he's happily married with three children. I really appreciate that. I prefer having a therapist who has a happy marriage. It just makes a difference to me. So I really lucked out."

"Well then, let the therapy begin. Let's celebrate and go out for dinner."

~~~

With a plan in place—to wrestle with my fears and insecurities about my marriage under the care of a professional therapist—I was ready to learn how to take one step at a time, one day at a time.

I clung to the terminology of "same-gender feelings"— those were Victor's words—because that seemed far less threatening than picturing Victor as someone who actually thinks he's gay. *Feelings come and go, right?* I reasoned. It's like the story in the Bible about the foolish man who builds his house upon the sand, instead of rock. Feelings are elusive; they're like grains of sand blowing in the wind. Anything based on feelings alone is likely to crumble and wash away, unsuitable material to support an enduring structure. I certainly had little regard for my own feelings; I was in survival mode, without the luxury of indulging in such feelings. I had learned as a young girl to keep my feelings to myself. I didn't know what to do with them. No one wanted to deal with my feelings, including me. So I dismissed my feelings as irrelevant and made them evaporate, disappear. I used my mind, not my emotions, to navigate through the maze of my circumstances.

Growing up in a family bombarded with extraordinary hardships in Vermont, I was surrounded by emotional upheaval during my childhood. When I was five years old, my sister became ill and died of leukemia at 14 years of age—an unbearable loss that devastated my family, especially my parents. My brother struggled with a profound social phobia (years later named "selective mutism")—he used me, his younger sister, as his mouthpiece and shield for others in the family (except my mother), and outside the family. My mother had issues—she was totally burned out on the demands of motherhood by the time I, the youngest of five children, was born.

When I was 12 years old, my world fell apart. My father was the rock in my life who always made me feel precious and grounded me in the teachings of Jesus and the ways of our evangelical church (those were the days when "evangelical" was an adjective to describe one's faith as a disciple of Jesus, not a type of voter). But his health went downhill fast, and he died of cancer within three months of diagnosis—too far gone for any treatments available at that time for his rare combination of leukemia and Hodgkin's disease. A forever Daddy's girl, I was heartbroken beyond repair. And my mother, overwhelmed with deep-seated anxieties and depression as well as jarring discoveries in her newfound freedom as a 50-year-old widow, could barely take care of herself, let alone me. Her needs and fears came first. My two older sisters had grown up and moved away. I was left on my own to fend for myself, ill-equipped to work through my emotions. I was a loner and turned to books and academic pursuits, seeking God's will for me.

I developed into a young woman of understated feelings, which I now can see is a major understatement.

When Victor came into my life, I began to blossom. I found Victor's love, attention, and passion irresistible. He cared about my feelings, my goals, my mind, my body—he embraced everything about me. I did the same for him. We built a strong marriage. We depended on each other. Without Victor, I could only imagine myself adrift without an anchor, losing my way, alone without anyone. Without Victor, I believed my life would have no meaning, purpose, or pleasure. I was desperate to hang onto him and our life together.

No way was I giving up on Victor and our God-ordained marriage. *We'll stick together through it all,* I told myself. We didn't have one of those throwaway marriages; I believed peanut butter was still left in the jar. I was confident if we could honestly face Victor's same-gender feelings, we would overcome any obstacles this threat posed and end up with an even stronger marriage in the end. *Love conquers all, right?*

~~~

I began to jot down thoughts and questions in a journal, hoping the act of writing would empty my mind of the incessant demands to make sense of it all. As a trained reporter, it was natural for me to come up with structured interview questions for Victor. I collected my ideas over the next two weeks and decided to "schedule an appointment" with Victor for a heart-to-heart talk (no alcohol allowed!) on a Saturday afternoon.

I was ready to have a serious conversation with Victor. I wanted to be the one in control of asking the questions and then listen carefully to everything he said. Looking back, perhaps this interview approach was my way of trying to look at our situation in an objective manner without making any judgments. I was hoping his responses would help me better understand his thoughts and feelings. Above all, I wanted him to know I was still on his side as he wrestled with his same-gender feelings.

I could see Victor had his own way of preparing for our conversation, pacing back and forth but keeping his promise that alcohol wouldn't interfere with our conversation and making sure Champ wouldn't be a distraction. After Victor had an energetic romp playing fetch with Champ around the house, the dog settled down and focused on ripping her plastic squeaky toy apart with her teeth while Victor and I sat in the Things-To-Do room for our talk. I clutched my notebook to my chest, bracing for what Victor might say.

"Okay, I wrote out some questions. I don't want to be an ostrich and bury my head in the sand, hoping all this will just go away."

"You can always talk about anything with me," he said as he fiddled with his moustache with what used to be his cigarette-smoking fingers to take in the faint smell he imagined from the tobacco stains that lingered. "So, what do you want to know?"

"This may seem awkward, with me reading interview questions like I do at work."

"Go ahead. Shoot me a question."

I lowered my notebook to my lap and started reading aloud.

"Question one: How would you describe the events of the last two weeks?"

"It's been hard on you, but rather liberating for me. I no longer have to keep my same-gender feelings a deep, dark secret from you."

So far, so good, I coached myself. I was encouraged by the tone of his first response: honest and direct. I took a deep breath and read the next question.

"Here's a multiple choice. Which statement best describes you right now?
A. I'm trying to figure out if I'm heterosexual or homosexual.
B. My sexual desire to be with a man or a woman is equally strong.
C. I know in my bones I'm gay."
He winced, then shrugged his shoulders. "None of the above. How about another question?"
"Okay," I said, puzzled by his dodge. "How would you visualize your life being different in a love relationship with a man? What can a man offer that a woman can't?"
"Well, that's an interesting question, but I don't have an interesting answer for that one right now."
I glanced down at my notebook, determined to keep our talk on track.
"Next question: Regarding the torment of knowing not a single day goes by when you don't have strong feelings to be sexually bonded with a man, how do you handle these feelings?"
"Truthfully, I have an active imagination," he said. "Most men I know are so homophobic—it's out of the question to show any affection. Lots of my friends grew up with fathers like mine, who rarely showed any physical affection. So I keep my feelings to myself."
"Well, that was sort of an answer. Next question: Do you believe real-life experiences can ever match the intensity of sexual fantasies?"
"I don't know. What do you think?"
"I think one's imagination is greater than reality," I said. "But I'm not really sure. Sexual fantasy isn't way up on my priority list these days. I'm too busy thinking up these questions, I guess. So here's another: Do you ever lie to me?"
"No."
"Why not?"
"Because I just don't lie to you."
"Isn't withholding the truth a form of lying?"

He flinched and said, "I don't see it that way."

"Really?"

I paused, caught off guard by his resistance to be more forthcoming. *Don't rock the boat,* I chastised myself. I planned this as a fact-finding mission, not a confrontation; I was digging for some answers. My job was to ask questions and listen; "first learn, then form opinions"—I believed in the wisdom of this Jewish proverb.

"Let's move on. Question seven: Do you feel in complete control of your actions at all times?"

"Yes, I don't do anything I don't want to do."

I had wondered if Victor was under the influence of someone else coaching him to explore his same-sex feelings by acting on them without telling me or using drugs or alcohol to overcome any inhibitions he had. Was he a target of someone's predatory motives? But his unwavering response debunked that possibility.

"Next question: How would you feel if I decided, in your words, 'to be open for sexual experiences' with other people? Would you want to know about it?"

"I just can't imagine you doing that," he said. "Even if you did, you'd certainly tell me all about it."

"Yes, I would," I said, trying to make it clear I expected him to be honest with me as much as he expected honesty from me at all times.

"Next question: Do you think bisexuality can often be a temporary transition between homosexuality and hetero-sexuality or heterosexuality and homosexuality? At the core, are people either gay or straight?"

"I don't know."

I was hoping this question would jumpstart a conversation about the complex nature of sexual orientation. But he slammed the door on that topic.

"So here's an important question: On a scale of 1 to 100—where 1 equals 100 percent homosexual and 100 equals 100 percent heterosexual—where do you consider yourself?"

"I can't answer that," he declared.

I couldn't believe he refused that question, which was so important to me. I wanted some metrics. It was a standard question that appears in many studies by Masters and Johnson, pioneers in the field of human sexual response: Victor and I had read their textbooks in college. I dismissed my disappointment and continued to probe.

"I've been reading how sexual orientation exists along a continuum. Plenty of people don't act on their same-gender feelings. Victor, can't you give me an honest answer?"

"No."

"Why not?"

Silence.

I backed off. Was Victor trying to protect me? Did he think I wasn't strong enough yet to handle an honest answer? Or was my question too harsh for someone who was grappling with sexual orientation issues, as if measures for sexual orientation, like pain thresholds, could be assigned?

"Okay, let's turn to some other questions. In your opinion, what's made our relationship special over the last 15 years?"

"We love each other. We're there for each other."

"And what do you find simply intolerable about me?"

"Nothing." He grinned. "You do ask a lot of questions at times—but nothing about you is intolerable."

I was grateful for his reassurance. But, in general, I was baffled by his responses to most of my questions; this talk raised more questions than it answered. Still, I plodded on with my final prepared questions.

"Next question: In your opinion, how does a person stop loving someone?"

"I don't know...." His voice faded away.

"Do you think it's conceivable for us to remain best friends but not married?"

"I pray we'll be best friends for eternity."

He sounded sincere, full of love for me.

"And what would it mean to you if our relationship came to an end?"

"It would be terrible. I want you in my life—always."

I felt the same way. Victor was my best friend. I didn't want to lose him.

"Victor, is this all about you having a mid-life crisis? Could all this be a variation on the theme that 'life is passing by, and you expected so much more'?"

"Not really. I don't think buying a Mercedes-Benz 450SL convertible is the cure for me."

"I want so much to make you happy. My last question: What can I do to become more sexually attractive to you?"

"There's nothing wrong with you. You don't have to change anything. Now can we have a drink?"

Chapter 5

"Christ is risen!" said Victor, as he leaned over my side of the bed to kiss me for our traditional Easter morning wake-up greeting.

"Christ is risen indeed!" I said, responsively, mustering up a joyful mood to start the day, with Champ full of dog licks and spunk at our side.

We arose, rolled away our bedding, and showered.

Resurrection was precisely what our marriage needed, too. *Help us crucify the uncertainty and chaos surrounding Victor's same-gender feelings and bring new life to our relationship*, I silently prayed as I dressed for the Easter church service.

Victor and I went to church together, holding hands. Pastor Norman gave an inspiring sermon and greeted us with two-handed handshakes as we left the church. We then traveled to see Victor's parents, a 45-minute drive, for an Easter celebration, Italian-style, with his extended family.

"Shall we play 'Let's-Pretend-Nothing's-Wrong-With-Our-Marriage' during this visit?" I asked Victor as we pulled in the driveway of his parents' upscale suburban home. "Or shall we add a bit of drama with the news we're under the care of professional therapists?"

"Fat chance," he said as he turned off the car's engine, yanked on the parking brake, and removed the key. "It's Easter. Let's be festive. I certainly have no plans to spill the beans about your St. Patrick's Day meltdown."

My meltdown?

I was somewhat annoyed but resisted the urge to debate his description of what actually happened that night. I didn't want to argue about it on Easter.

When I had made a solo trip the previous weekend to visit my own family of origin—yes, that's the language I've picked up in therapy—I was surprised to see how easy it was to put aside my issues. I didn't say a word about the major fracture in our marriage. I was too busy trying to figure out the latest nonsense in their lives. I expected the same from Victor's family. Being an "outsider" daughter-in-law seemed to offer immunity from participation in the yelling matches, which focused more on external issues than internal crises. I was grateful they usually left me off their list of grievances against others.

~~~

Victor's family went all out for the holidays. His mother, who isn't even Italian, had labored all week as a front-desk clerk at the local post office and then worked her tail off to prepare an Italian feast. His father, a self-employed master carpenter—yes, Victor, like Jesus, was the son of a carpenter—was full of old-world Italian charm toward me. He has always taken delight in my hearty appetite, teasing me to *"Mangia, mangia"* when the food's served in heaping portions. Victor's parents were so proud of us, our happy marriage, and our jobs.

As usual, the Easter celebration was a big production—with Aunt Angelina's Easter rice pie, hot cross buns, honey-pineapple glazed ham, lasagna (as a side dish), and a few token vegetables that comply with Weight Watchers for the diet-conscious members of the family, along with cheesecake, cannolis, fresh-brewed coffee, and a nip of Anisette for dessert.

Victor's family focused on the food, not us. We played with our nieces and nephews while the adults bantered and complained about their work, their bosses, other relatives, and world events. We made a graceful exit after the festivities, believing no one had a clue trouble was brewing in our marriage.

With a sense of relief, we headed back home. While Victor was driving, we let loose and began to sing, a cappella, "This Is the Day That the Lord Has Made." We were in a joyful mood; the acoustics in our small car had a similar effect as singing in the shower—it made us sound better than we actually were. So we continued our spontaneous songfest with Easter-themed hymns: "Christ the Lord Is Risen Today, Alleluia"; "He Arose" (singing with added gusto when we reached the part about "He arose a Victor from the dark domain"); "I Serve a Risen Savior, He's in the World Today"; and "O Sacred Head, Now Wounded, With Grief and Shame Weighed Down"—but neither of us could remember the words for that one so we sang the rest of the tune with "la la la."

For our finale, we sang "Because He Lives" in harmony; Victor took the lead, and I sang alto. Singing this song together made me feel nostalgic about how we used to find meaning in focusing on the needs of others, rather than dwelling on our own self-absorbed issues.

"Remember our college days when we went to the nursing home on Sundays to cheer up all those lonely-looking people with this song?" I asked.

"I sure do. We made a big hit with this song, after people turned down their hearing aids."

We both chuckled.

"But they told us they liked the old-fashioned hymns more than the modern songs," I said.

"Speaking of modern songs, let's do some Dylan."

He popped in his cassette tape of *Slow Train Coming,* and we sang along.

"Dylan's a genius," he said. "Every song on this album is a masterpiece."

I stared out the car window, weighing our recent progress to myself. Victor had started seeing a psychiatrist on a monthly basis. He told me he liked talking with Dr. Boland, an older woman in private practice who monitored the effectiveness of his antidepressant. He also had taken the initiative to find a men's support group led by a male counselor, hoping to connect with other men interested in discussing self-growth issues. He said they didn't beat drums *a la* Robert Bly and his book, *Iron John*, but they did explore issues relating to "tapping into warrior energy" and "being a man" in today's world. He told me sex was a popular topic of discussion, but no one seemed to show much interest in talking about any "same-gender feelings." The bottom line: So far it seemed these efforts weren't meeting Victor's core needs in coming to terms with his hunger for more masculinity in his life.

I was discouraged about his slow progress in moving beyond inertia; I was hoping Victor would work through his same-gender feelings and come to the conclusion that his yearnings were more psychological than sexual. It could be male bonding without any same-gender sexual activity was really what Victor needed in his life. Perhaps he just needed more time to sort things out.

I closed my eyes and pictured a train—a huge, thundering freight train with clouds of smoke billowing overhead, loaded with all the heavy burdens we were hauling around. Were Victor and I on the right track, headed in the right direction? Was I a victim of my own tendency to worry needlessly over a situation that would all work out in the end? Or were we procrastinating, avoiding realities and failing to move on?

Slow train coming indeed!

~~~

Our lives did chug along. Victor and I continued to coexist compatibly, focusing on our work and spending most of our time outside of work together. However, our relationship started to evolve into a series of connects and disconnects, whereas before Victor's revelation on St. Patrick's Day, it seemed we lived in a perpetual state of connection.

37

The following Saturday morning I was scheduled to work in the local family planning clinic, something I enjoyed doing once a month. The pay was low, but the work was satisfying and provided an outlet for my strong commitment to women's issues, as well as a way to stay in touch with my training and skills as a social worker. I was very good at helping women, especially teenagers, feel comfortable in the family planning clinic, offering concrete services to promote responsible decision-making about their health and contraception. Empathy and nonjudgmental regard toward each person who came to the clinic were the cornerstones of my interactions; I made it my career to be nonjudgmental.

But after I arrived at the clinic, I discovered we were overstaffed that day so I offered to leave and drove back home.

After parking the car in our driveway, I unlocked the front door and shouted out to Victor, "Surprise! I'm home." As I headed through the kitchen to the family room, with Champ yapping at my heels, I saw Victor on the carpet with his legs spread wide apart and his back up against the side of the armchair, positioned in front of a blank TV screen with a bottle of Bertolli Extra Virgin Olive Oil on one side and the VCR remote control on the other side of him. He was naked except for a small towel thrown over his privates.

"Oh," I said, quickly sizing up the situation and wanting to make this scene less awkward for Victor. "I see I'm back in time for some fun."

I slipped out of my clothes and slithered down on the carpet next to him.

"I assume this is more fun with me than without me, right?"

"Well—," he said.

"Well what?"

"I wasn't expecting you back so soon."

"The clinic was overstaffed today so I decided not to stick around and instead came home to be with you. So watcha watching? Saturday morning cartoons?"

"Not exactly. You know, it's really embarrassing, you walking in on me like this."

I had often told Victor how glad I was to have a husband who could take care of his own sexual needs all by himself, especially when I wasn't around. I considered an active masturbation life as a good thing as long as it didn't interfere with the way we related to each other.

"So you wanna see what I'm watching?" he said.

His words came across as a dare, as if my open-minded sensibilities were on trial.

"If you want me to," I said, showing my willingness to take the dare.

He pressed the Play button on the VCR remote control, and we watched about a minute of his video. A couple of grown men, naked with erections, were posing for each other on the branches of a tree.

"Whoa," I said. "That's enough for me. This is some sort of gay porn?"

"It's a matter of curiosity for me."

He pushed the Stop button and then ejected the tape.

"Outdoor sex? That's certainly a possibility," I said, grasping for something redeeming about this disturbing scene. "Splendor in the grass? Yes. Climbing a tree, barefoot and butt naked? No way. I think I need to get dressed now and do something else with my day."

I rounded up my clothes and clutched them to my body as I stood up and left the room. Was this a constructive way for Victor to explore his same-gender feelings? Or was it a tool to nurture hedonistic behavior, a prelude for acting on his feelings? Where and when did he find gay pornography? I hated the thought this video was in our home, making me fearful of Victor's descent to the dark domain leading to the demise of our marriage. This was my competition for Victor's sexual attention? But I coached myself: *Be nonjudgmental. Don't drive Victor away by showing any intolerance toward his soul-searching journey of self-growth.* I was struggling with conflicts of my own: How could I show my husband I accept him just as he is, along with his same-gender feelings, when they posed such a threat to our marriage? How could we continue to have a marriage that is satisfying for both of us? Flabbergasted, I switched my emotional gears to numbness. I decided to file it away for my next session with Dr. Barley. I refused to let it ruin my day.

"Okay. Me, too," said Victor, his voice chasing me as I walked upstairs. "Hey, let's go for a bike ride together."

Chapter 6

Cycling had become the major outdoor activity Victor and I did together, other than walking Champ with a leash on the sidewalks around our neighborhood in the evening and on weekends. Although Victor was far more athletic than me—with almost daily workouts at his company's fitness center, tennis with his friends, and a history of jogging inspired by Jim Fixx's books in the 1980s—I found time on occasion to go along on his "easy rides" within a 10-mile radius of our home on the flat landscapes of Somerset County. Victor rode a nifty racing bicycle with drop handlebars, while I pedaled my old-fashioned, three-speed Schwinn bike we had bought at a yard sale.

Both Victor and I struggled to maintain healthy body weights; when we first met, we were "butterballs"—tipping the scales well over 200 pounds each. As a teenager, Victor fit the definition of "husky"—he had the photos to prove it—and I was chubby most of my life since fifth grade. Gym class in school was a nightmare for both of us; any participation in team sports was unrelenting torture, not fun. We had zero interest as spectators of any sport, unless a friend or relative needed a cheerleading squad; we knew how to shout out "Give it your best shot!" and "Way to go!" We did watch the Olympics on TV every four years because it was irresistible to see trained athletes experience "the thrill of victory…and the agony of defeat," just like the rest of the nonathletic universe.

As teenagers, we found great comfort in food—consuming tons of ice cream and baked goods—perhaps to fill the emotional emptiness we felt growing up. During the months before our wedding, we both dieted strenuously to reach our ideal weights, convincing ourselves that people who are in love have access to all the affection and support needed from one another instead of food. We broke the chains of food tyranny together.

We became vegetarians in our early 30s, after reading the controversial book by Harvey and Marilyn Diamond called *Fit for Life* (written before they divorced). No longer eating "cooked flesh" made us feel better; we were nonproselytizing vegetarians, tolerant of meat eaters but not serving any meat, chicken, or fish in our home. Only Champ, a carnivore, was allowed her daily canned dog food. Our approach to reeducating ourselves about the role of food worked for us throughout our marriage, with periodic yo-yo weight gains and losses kept in check for the most part.

Victor regarded exercise as an effective outlet to help curb his cravings for nicotine, as well as to help control his weight. I was so proud of him: He had quit smoking cigarettes! Life was so much better without ashtrays, smoker's breath, and hacking coughs. Cycling helped build endurance and was less intense than jogging. After long nights of hard drinking, mounting a bicycle was more doable for him the morning after than taking a run in the countryside without tripping.

For me, not only did my therapist, Dr. Barley, strongly recommend exercise for mental health reasons because "exercise increases serotonin levels to combat depression," but I embraced cycling as a metaphor for my life, meditating on Albert Einstein's observation that "life is like riding a bicycle—in order to keep your balance, you must keep moving."

~~~

That's how I lived my life. I just kept moving. Not only was my job a welcome distraction to the struggles in my marriage, but it provided never-ending fascination by challenging me with intellectual stimulation and sharpening my interpersonal skills, along with frequent business trips to attend Foundation meetings to interact with grantees. I loved every minute of it.

I was absorbed in the work of the Foundation in communicating "lessons learned" through its investments in helping community organizations, as well as policymakers, deal with the HIV/AIDS epidemic. I was assigned to serve a role in the editing work of three important communication tools: the proceedings of an HIV/AIDS conference held in Washington, DC (a special project that the Foundation's President wanted completed within six months); a book targeting what Americans can do about HIV/AIDS at the community level; and a newspaper-format publication that provided highlights from effective Foundation-supported initiatives in this area.

Conscientious in doing my homework, I read *And the Band Played On* by Randy Shilts from cover to cover for background purposes. Published in 1987, this tome of a book chronicled the AIDS epidemic during its early years, including some eye-opening descriptions on the lives of gay men in the bathhouses of San Francisco. No way could I picture Victor having the slightest interest whatsoever in the sordid details of such gay orgies. I somehow was able to focus with compassion on the tragedies of everyone else confronting the realities of HIV/AIDS, dismissing any relevance to the possibilities of Victor becoming part of the future story of the epidemic.

My knowledge expanded in all areas of health policy, including children's health, health care for homeless families, health issues of minority groups, improving the health of Native Americans, mental health services for youth, caregiver programs to assist people with disabilities and the elderly, quality of care issues, research and evaluation initiatives, strengthening the American healthcare workforce, and long-term care insurance programs. I made day trips to New York City and Philadelphia, as well as more extensive travel to Washington, DC, and Chicago.

In early June, I conducted a string of intensive face-to-face interviews with various grantees over three days, meeting with a grantee working with street prostitutes in Denver, Colorado, on Monday afternoon; taking a flight to Los Angeles later that night to meet with grantees working with homeless people on Tuesday; and then capping my West Coast trip with a visit to San Francisco on Tuesday evening to meet with more grantees on Wednesday. The Foundation's travel agent always made sure my accommodations placed safety first. However, I must confess it felt strange to choose from the five dining rooms at The Fairmont for an elegant dinner with a violinist serenading me tableside while writing up my notes about organizations serving homeless populations; later I slept in a well-appointed hotel room with an extra empty bed. I was moved by the work of people who cared about others without adequate food and shelter, yet there I was eating and sleeping in luxurious surroundings.

I was no stranger to cognitive dissonance, having an uncomfortable feeling about holding two contradictory ideas simultaneously—namely, caring about the homeless but not sharing my resources at hand. Such irony triggered other thoughts: How could someone (namely, Victor) or something (namely, our marriage) come across as being one thing and turn out to be something else all along? Why was everything so complicated? What could be done to make everything right? I had no answers. I preferred to focus on my job.

My work schedule included attending Foundation teas, dinners, and celebration events—always cognizant of my role as an ambassador for my employer. I lived in a perpetual sponge mode, soaking up as much information as possible to become conversant about serious health issues that Americans face. My workload included preparing program summaries and other communications infrastructure work. I tried to be a useful resource to everyone I encountered.

I also was able to choose my own secretary—a fashion-conscious woman with a flair for making my letters and other documents look flawless who managed my travel and appointment calendar, screened my telephone calls, executed mail merges, and did my filing. I worked in an office (not a cubicle!) with a window and brand-new oak furniture. I will never forget the day the Foundation's President stopped by my office to shake my hand to congratulate me on my work on the proceedings publication. I was thrilled he took the time to learn my name, and I received a credit line as the editor of this book.

My work life was a welcome distraction to my home life. I bonded with people at work, extending every courtesy possible to all of my coworkers throughout the Foundation. Some of the VIPs could be a bit intimidating, but I did my best to defer without coming across as too patronizing; I was a team player enthralled with working in the foundation world. I developed a reputation for being positive, dependable, and hard-working, as well as a good listener, observer, and notetaker. I considered it an amazing privilege to be part of this Foundation's family.

Yet, while my work was becoming an anchor for me, my marriage was teetering on the fence of uncertainty, making very little progress with Victor's "daily torture." Although things appeared on the surface to be okay, a gnawing undercurrent of strain had become a way of life.

~~~

Of all things, a segment on the TV show "Face to Face With Connie Chung" in early September 1990 shook me up. It had been six months since Victor's admission about his same-gender feelings. The lead story that Sunday night was a 10-minute profile about sexual trysts among bisexual and gay men at highway rest areas. The key message was these men rarely consider themselves at risk for HIV/AIDS transmission and consequently don't take safer sex precautions. Victor and I watched the program together in silence and then tumbled into bed upstairs. I had a somewhat eerie yet unfounded feeling that Victor already knew about rest areas as a meeting place for sex among strangers.

Ten minutes later as we were lying side by side in the darkness of our bedroom, I decided to bring it up.

"I know this may sound crazy—"

"Go on. You can say it," said Victor, as if he already knew what I was going to say.

"It's really scary for me to think you're asking yourself questions about your sexual orientation," I said, choosing my words carefully. "I'm scared you could fall into the sort of trap we watched on TV tonight."

After an extended period of silence, Victor reached for the lamp on the nightstand on his side of the bed and turned it on.

"You know this issue has yet to be resolved," he said. "I know you have such mixed feelings about me."

"I'm trying to tell you how I feel about watching that program," I said, hoping that talking about it would keep me from letting my fearful thoughts turn to irrational obsession. "You need to be patient with me."

Silence.

"How does it make you feel when I'm like this?" I asked.

"Actually, I'm frustrated," said Victor.

"Tell me more. I need to know how you feel about me."

"I made a big mistake when I told you about my same-gender feelings back in March," said Victor. "I'm afraid what will happen to us. I wonder if you'll ever be able to forgive me."

"You mean forgive you for having these same-gender feelings or forgive you for hiding them from me?"

"There you go again, dissecting everything I say," he said.

I was confused and continued to struggle in separating my unconditional regard for Victor's same-gender feelings as a basic human right for all people from my fear of being married to a man who might turn out to be gay.

"Honesty is the only way to get through this. I love you, Victor, and I accept you as being the person you are."

46

"This is *my* issue. This is *my* problem. I don't know why you insist on making it your problem," he shot back at me, beating his fist on the bed.

"I know it's *your* issue and *your* problem. But it also affects me. I'm scared. I need to learn how to live with this issue."

He glared at me.

"What exactly do you fear, Vivian?"

"I don't want to lose you. I feel so vulnerable."

He softened his gaze and then cupped his head with his clasped hands as he leaned back on his pillow.

"So what do we do?"

"I don't know," I said, bewildered by the enormous complexities of Victor's issues. I decided from that point on I would remove myself from any disturbing TV shows, discussions, and situations that could feed my fears about our marriage. Who would guess a report by Connie Chung would trigger such pillow talk?

Victor turned off the light and then rolled over so his back was toward me, signaling the end of our conversation.

Chapter 7

"Riddled with anxiety" was a phrase Victor and I often used to describe ourselves during particularly stressful times. I would picture a scene from a TV crime show after a SWAT team pummeled a target with an extended round of gunfire, leaving a wall riddled with bullets. That's how I felt—with anxiety splattered all around me.

Fortunately, I was learning many new insights about myself in therapy. For starters, my fears and obsessions were legion. Fear of abandonment, fear of failure (which I defined as failing to meet my expectations and/or the expectations of others), fear of saying the wrong words and being misunderstood, and fear of losing control and going off the deep end were among my top fears. Above all, the fear of not being loved was my number one fear. That, along with my subzero self-esteem, made the thought of living without Victor terrifying.

I can credit my mother for instilling these anxieties in me from an early age, propagated by her core beliefs: *You aren't allowed to have or express uncomfortable feelings, such as anger or sadness; whatever you do, don't hurt anyone's feelings, which is the worst thing you could ever do;* and *all men are beasts.* I had disproved the notion of "all men are beasts" by having Victor in my life. But her other two beliefs seemed to be hardwired into my psyche, which didn't serve me well.

Early on in our work, my therapist posed the question, "Vivian, wouldn't it be liberating to live one day of your life free from fear or obsession?" I was dumbfounded by this thought. What a concept! Just one day free from fear or obsession? I didn't have a clue how to do that.

Yet, the burdens of growing sleeplessness due to late night mind racing and continual exhaustion were beginning to take their toll. Why not consider medication? I had constructed a rationale to avoid prescription drugs at that time. First, I decided taking an antidepressant signals an admission I'm in serious trouble; I was willing to acknowledge my issues were serious and my circumstances were troubling, but not necessarily that I was in serious trouble. Second, I thought medication use was the beginning of a psychiatric history, which would scar me for life. Third, I was concerned an antidepressant would mask my feelings; it was difficult enough for me to identify my feelings and really feel them without medication. Fourth, I was concerned about creating long-term dependence. Fifth, I didn't trust myself to steer clear from abusing any medication.

On the other hand, why not accept any help to ease my pain and relieve my anxiety? Victor seemed to think combining his antidepressant with daily alcohol use worked just fine for him. He was a man of activity more than a man of introspection. My approach to self-actualization was to think things through, gather more information, and read some books. And I still believed in the power of prayer. However, I decided I would trust my therapist's judgment: If Dr. Barley were to tell me medication use was imperative, I would comply.

~~~

The following Saturday, Victor and I decided to embark on a 20-mile cycling adventure. Victor had bought himself a spanking new, 10-speed mountain bike that week and was eager to take it for a ride. He suggested I ride along using his racing bike, which would make it easier for me to keep up with him. He also purchased a matching pair of "serious cycling pants" for me and himself—they were black, sleek, and stretchy as well as great fun to wear once we tugged them on. I was glad Victor wanted me to discover the joy of riding bikes together.

Before we started the ride on this brisk day, Victor offered me some gear-shifting and pedal-pacing advice. I acknowledged his suggestions and reminded him, "This is still all new to me, but I'll try my best." We strapped on our new bike helmets and started out riding side by side.

This bike ride feels good, I said to myself. *Perhaps this is the day I can find out how liberating it can be to live one day of my life free from fear or obsession.* Despite a quicker pace than last week, I was able to hold my own and keep up with Victor. He was leading the way because I had never traveled on these one-lane back roads with sparse signage.

Twenty minutes into the ride, our downhill speeds and multiple curves kept me from having Victor ahead in view. *No big deal—I'm sure as soon as a long stretch or uphill climb comes up, he'll be in sight,* I coached myself.

Another 20 minutes went by. No sign of Victor. I started to wonder, why wasn't Victor concerned about me? Wasn't this supposed to be a "togetherness activity"?

I pedaled a little faster, hoping I wasn't missing any turnoffs and beginning to feel annoyed about how this was turning into a "solo" event. I started to realize I was on my way to becoming lost, in the middle of nowhere with no sense of direction. I was unsure how to backtrack and find my way home. I began to panic. How foolish of me to have no map or directions for this ride! I saw no landmarks to figure out my bearings and no one to ask for help. And worse yet, I couldn't count on Victor to show me the way. Whatever happened to the Victor who adored being with me all the time and cared more about me than he cared about himself? My blind faith in him had let me down.

Then, out of the blue, he rode up from behind me.

"Hey, I spotted an off-the-road trail that was irresistible. So I just had to explore it. By the way, I see you're not shifting the gears on my racing bike the way I told you. Can't you do better than that?"

I was hurt and confused by his lack of concern about me feeling left behind. But I didn't want to annoy him with my whining and complaining. I focused on trying to help him understand my perspective.

"I had no idea where you were," I said. "You just disappeared all of a sudden, leaving me behind in the dust. And I have no idea which roads to take."

"Oh, I bet you probably thought I had gone off and left you for good," Victor joked sadistically as he broke into laughter.

"Go ahead and make fun of me and my issues. That's really helpful."

He stopped laughing.

"Hey, why don't we pull over and rest a few minutes?"

"No, I insist on going on," I said, in tears at that point and wanting to avoid turning this "togetherness venture" into a big drama. "Please show me the way back home, now. And keep checking to make sure I'm right behind you."

We cut the ride short by taking a different loop. We pedaled in silence and arrived home an hour later. I was afraid Victor would think I was a party pooper even though I thought I was being a good sport to put up with his antics. I decided I would let him know later that I didn't appreciate his attitude.

After we dismounted our bikes, squeezed out of our clothes, and showered, I spoke my mind.

"I feel better now. But you really hurt my feelings. You know cycling is all new to me. I'm working hard and doing my best. You should be encouraging me, not criticizing me and poking fun at me."

"Oh, come on. I thought I was being encouraging."

"You were encouraging in the beginning, but things turned sour."

"Well, I'm sorry I hurt your feelings. But don't be so sensitive. I love my new bike. I'm looking forward to lots of new adventures. I'm having a blast."

Was this bike outing Victor's way of teaching me not to count on him to lead me through unknown territory? Was he following some kind of manual on how to make his wife a nervous wreck? Was he giving me some practice in no longer trusting him to do the right thing? Was he plotting how to go his own way, leaving me behind to fend for myself? Was I blowing this way out of proportion and overthinking an innocent incident? But I didn't share any of these thoughts with Victor. I was afraid he would accuse me of looking for trouble and being a killjoy.

I started to develop a new way of thinking: Wherever he leads, I might not follow. I had never had this thought before about Victor. Was I developing a streak of rebellion? But then I dismissed this line of thinking and decided to be like Mary, recalling the Bible verse about how she reacted under different circumstances when she "kept all these things, pondering them in her heart" (Luke 2:19, RSV).

~~~

Two months later, on the day after Thanksgiving, Victor announced he had a big surprise for me—an early Christmas present. He drove me to a store 15 miles away and presented me with a shiny, 20-inch, teal, 10-speed Raleigh mountain bike. He was excited about giving me a new bike of my own. I think he had high hopes for me to be his mountain bike buddy. I regarded it as a peace offering, as well as a vote of confidence in my ability to learn how to ride over rough terrain. Perhaps he wanted me to channel my extreme anxiety about our marriage into something constructive: exercise. After inviting me to take it for a spin around the parking lot to see if I liked the way it handled, he whipped out his VISA card to purchase the $430 bike. I went along with this idea, noting the model name of this bike was perfect for me; emblazoned at crotch level on the top tube of the bike in white lettering was the word *Obsession*.

Chapter 8

Let go, let go, let go—these words were my mantra, while driving in the car alone, sitting through long meetings at work, doing household chores, riding my bike, and taking Champ for a walk. That was the mindset I needed to release my relentless worrying about Victor and our marriage. I tried to visualize making my personal anxieties rise up and drift away on clouds, as if on parade. I knew from my Bible that I needed to "cast your burden on the Lord, and he will sustain you" (Psalm 55:22, RSV) so I prayed, asking God to take away the pain and uncertainty. But God felt mighty distant these days, and I could see no way out of this heartbreak and inertia.

So I "girded up my loins"—which is Biblespeak for when a person summons inner resources in preparation for action—with new resolve to take control of my own issues. With encouragement from my therapist, I tried to describe my "bundle of mixed feelings"—compiling a rather long list in bullet form:

• I feel discouraged about my progress in "letting go" and moving beyond my emotional dependency on Victor.

• I feel perplexed and bewildered by Victor's perception that I have not been "in the least bit understanding" of his thoughts and feelings during the past seven months.

• I feel neglected when Victor seems to have no patience or interest in listening to me. Sometimes when he is so preoccupied with his own self-centered circumstances, I feel like grabbing him by the arms and screaming, "Victor, get interested in *me*."

• I feel unaffirmed, unattractive, and undesirable when Victor's sexual interest isn't directed toward me.

- I feel anxious and apprehensive whenever Victor gives me his cold, stern glare of anger or annoyance.
- I feel sad and empty inside whenever I think about uncertainties in the future and the possibility of living without Victor in my life.
- I feel distressed by the notion that Victor regards his fidelity commitment to me now in terms of martyrdom. (Doesn't martyrdom lead to resentment?)

That's all I could come up with in identifying my feelings. However, I wasn't done writing. I started to take inventory of how I was handling my situation and jotted down more thoughts, as if I was composing talking points for some sort of "State of Our Marital Union" address:

I feel I'm doing everything I can to be a loving and supportive wife:
- I took immediate action to begin therapy about my own personal needs and issues, including those related to my relationship with Victor.
- I'm following through with my commitment to ongoing therapy, trying to refocus my energy beyond "learning to cope" to "learning to grow" and creating a support system apart from Victor.
- I haven't launched any campaigns that attempt to undermine Victor. I didn't confide in anyone except my therapist and my pastor about Victor's same-gender feelings because I respect his privacy. I don't want to add more complications that could interfere as he works through his issues.
- I'm not judgmental toward Victor's feelings and, to the best of my ability, accept his need for more time to figure things out.
- I've communicated what I see as nonnegotiable issues in our marriage and have set clear boundaries about the consequences of infidelity.

• I make myself available to be a good listener at all times.

• I offer affirmation and encouragement to Victor about his personal growth.

• I try to avoid any behavior that can be construed as nagging, preaching, or putdowns of Victor. I don't make fun of his issues.

• I respect the privacy of Victor's work with his therapist and make no demands on him to share the content of his sessions.

• I don't engage in any "search and destroy" detective missions that seek to prove Victor may be violating our marriage vows or lying to me about his activities or whereabouts. I don't try to conspire with others to serve as spies or "Vivian advocates."

• I take the difficulties and challenges of our relationship seriously.

• I try not to burden Victor with endless discussions about my fears and bouts of depression.

• I remain committed to the preservation and growth of our marriage. I will do everything in my power to keep our marriage afloat.

• I feel the bond of love between us is strong enough and real enough to endure our difficulties. Although it's hard work for each of us to sort out our own complex issues, I believe we can move through this painful growth process, which will make us stronger as individuals and stronger as a couple.

~~~

I decided to show these pages of handwritten notes to Victor one night while sitting at the kitchen table after dinner. I was somewhat apprehensive, not knowing if he would be upset by the content or proud of me for trying to put my feelings into words. He flipped through and read page after page without comment.

"Well, this is really something," he said, glancing away from the pages to stare at me. "Is this some sort of progress report designed to put more pressure on me?"

"Quite the contrary. I'm simply describing my thoughts and feelings."

"So this is what you're doing in therapy," he said. "You and your therapist are ganging up to put me on some kind of guilt trip? You're really smothering me with all this psychobabble."

"Psychobabble? You're the one who majored in psychology."

"But I never thought I'd see the day when our relationship would be scrutinized in a therapist's office without any input from me."

"That's why I'm sharing this with you. I thought this would help you understand how I'm coping with all this."

"I don't know what you expect me to do," he said. "I keep telling you over and over. This is *my* issue. This is *my* problem. I am who I am. I don't know what will happen. I do know it doesn't help me to have people trying to push me over the edge."

"What edge? No one's trying to push you over any edge. I'm your wife. I'm doing my best to figure things out on my end. I want a happy ending for us."

"Then back off. Give me some space to breathe. And give me a break. This is really hard for me."

He tossed the envelope with my notes back at me across the table. He stood up and walked away from the kitchen, with a glass of Jack Daniel's, no ice, in his hands.

I felt misunderstood and frustrated. Perhaps it was better to keep my feelings to myself?

~~~

Later that week, Victor came home with a video he had rented, *The Last Temptation of Christ.* We had both read reviews of this controversial movie, which was based on the interpretation of a novel, not Scripture, and was considered offensive and blasphemous by many viewers. We agreed it was a haunting depiction of the crucifixion; the final section of the movie showed Jesus slowly dying on the cross, using a dream sequence in which He imagines a different life for himself—with sex (including same-gender feelings), sin, and hatred. Why did it seem as if my world had been taken over by all this fascination with same-gender sexual attraction? I pondered.

When we discussed the movie, it became clear that Victor liked the way Jesus was depicted as coming to terms with who He is and what He must do. I liked the part about how Jesus struggled to do God's will, without ever giving in to temptations of the flesh. Our different points of view seemed to reflect how we were handling our relationship: Victor was interested in identity issues whereas I was focused on overcoming threats to our marriage.

Furthermore, Victor loved the soundtrack by Peter Gabriel; he bought the recording and played it often. The sounds and rhythms of the soundtrack matched the brooding conflicts, tensions, and doubts depicted in the movie. I quickly developed an extreme aversion to this music. I told Victor listening to music such as "The Feeling Begins" track puts me in a bad mood. I didn't need any background music for thinking deeply about what makes us unhappy.

~~~

Despite these recent interactions, I managed to convince myself that Victor and I were doing the best we could do. On the surface, our relationship was more functional than dysfunctional. I made a conscious decision to adopt a "let it be" attitude, accept life as it was, and enjoy every ounce of meaning and pleasure in our relationship for as long as possible. I wanted to believe all we needed to do was stay calm and keep our marriage on a steady course forward. Besides, this was December—a time when it was easy to bury ourselves in the activities of Christmas.

Three days after Christmas, I struck up a conversation with Victor during a rather low-key evening at home.

"I'm making a New Year's resolution right now to prepare a less messy map about directions to our home. We can do better than the one we have now to help friends find their way here."

"That's a good idea," Victor mumbled, engrossed in a magazine.

"Any resolutions or expectations you have for 1991?" I asked.

"Not really," he said, flipping a page. "What about you?"

"I would like it to be a year for personal growth and for us to become closer. I do believe personal growth and growth as a couple can be compatible."

"Actually," said Victor as he slapped his magazine shut, "I declare 1991 will be the year we separate and I'll find a homosexual lover."

I froze, speechless. I wanted to believe Victor was joking, but it was hard to take his comment lightly because he had said exactly what I most feared.

"Oh, come on," he said. "You take everything so seriously. I'm just trying to show you how ridiculous you can be. You act like a helpless victim. I can't possibly meet all the needs you have. You better start dealing with all your issues. Let's face it. It's not working."

"It's not working? What does that mean?"

"It doesn't mean anything. They're just words."

I was confused. He was saying one thing, but asking me not to take his words literally.

"You really expect making that kind of statement will come across as a joke to me?" I said. "How can you be so cruel to me and keep jerking me around?"

"You're the one who's jerking yourself around. You have such a vivid imagination. And by the way, what I do in my private life by myself is my own business. I don't need you trying to dump any shame issues on me."

"Where did that come from?"

"You keep harping on me with questions like 'What's going on inside, Victor?' and 'What's going to happen with us?' Just the sound of your voice makes me want to scream sometimes."

"Well, go ahead and scream. I think that's what you're doing right now. If it makes you feel better, scream at me. They're just words, right?"

"Okay, let's calm down. Enough talk about resolutions, you know what I mean?"

"I guess so. I had no idea this conversation would lead to such a blowup. No more talk about resolutions. Ever."

This sudden volcanic eruption of emotions from Victor caught me totally off guard. His hostility seemed clear; a storm was brewing inside of him, beyond my control. I was afraid I would make him more upset by pointing it out to him. I resolved to make self-preservation my number one guiding principle from that day forward.

Chapter 9

The new year of 1991 started with the banging of pots and pans, the chopping of vegetables, and the whirring of our Cuisinart food processor. Victor and I were hard at work making our final preparations for a New Year's Day Open House. This was an annual tradition we started when we moved into our townhome—inviting all of our friends, neighbors, and family to celebrate new beginnings. Victor orchestrated the menu and did all the cooking—whipping up great-tasting vegetarian entrees—while I served as kitchen helper and scooted around the house with the vacuum cleaner one last time before our guests arrived. Even Champ could sense the unusual flurry of activity, trying her best to avoid being underfoot.

We expected anywhere from 30 to 50 people to stop by and served plenty of food and drink, buffet style. Full of charm and personality, Victor could really shine when entertaining others, using his extraordinary ability to make everyone feel welcomed by drawing out the quiet guests and reveling with the rowdy guests. I tried to follow his example of making everyone feel comfortable.

People did indeed show up as expected—even the undependable people in our lives. They came and went in unpredictable batches. As the official partying came to a close, our guests encouraged Victor and me to cap off the evening by playing duets on our Yamaha baby grand piano—a cherished possession we had purchased with the money we received from selling our bright yellow CJ-7 Jeep. Everyone at the party knew about our Jeep, which had given Victor an outlet for his daredevil impulses. We joked about how much money we saved by not having that Jeep anymore; we had believed that "a Jeep can do anything," but learned the hard way it doesn't do well driving on icy roads or straddling gullies on remote maple sugaring trails in Vermont. We spent lots of money replacing expensive tires whenever we took it off-road with the hard top removed. We gladly traded in our Jeep adventures for the thrill of this brand-new piano; even though our piano-playing skills were intermediate level at best, we practiced with great enthusiasm.

"How about playing some tunes for us?" said Alice, a former neighbor who continued to be a good friend after she, her husband, and their son moved into their dream home in the next county.

"That'll really chase everyone home," said Victor, with a chuckle. "But okay. Vivian, let's show 'em what we can do. It's duet time."

"Sure," I said, confident we could put on a show together.

We had a couple of duet books with four-handed arrangements but we could only play a few of them without hitting too many wrong notes. For example, we had been practicing "Stars and Stripes Forever," but we probably wouldn't be ready to perform that one for company until the Fourth of July.

"Ladies and gentlemen, our first number will be 'I Left My Heart in San Francisco,'" announced Victor. "If any Tony Bennett wannabes are in the room, feel free to sing along."

After we ended this song, polite applause encouraged us to tackle "Days of Wine and Roses" as a duet. And for the finale, we played the one we had practiced the most, "Breaking Up Is Hard to Do"—but we did a much slower-paced rendition than Neil Sedaka's original recording so we had a better chance of fitting in all the notes.

"Well done," said Alice. "But why such sad songs for such a happily married couple?"

Victor and I looked at each other and shrugged.

"Good question," I replied, not really appreciating at that time the irony of us working so hard to learn how to play a song about ending a romance. "I guess Victor and I are so focused on trying to play the right notes that we really don't think about the lyrics of these songs."

Victor had a better way of changing the subject: He suggested it was time to play some Bob Dylan records on the stereo. That was the cue for those who weren't Dylan fans to make their exit.

~~~

Later, when all the guests had left, Victor and I collapsed in happy exhaustion.

"What a party! You did a great job with all the food and hospitality," I said.

"*We* did a great job," said Victor. "Everything turned out well, and everybody seemed to have a good time. We are a great couple, you know."

"A couple of what—social misfits or gluttons for punishment?"

"A couple of really great people who know how to throw a good party."

I found it reassuring to work as a couple in making the open house a great success. We both valued our friends and family; we were grateful to have a home with enough space for such a celebration. I felt we were off to a great start for a new year, together, united for a purpose and caring for each another.

~~~

Victor and I focused most of our energy on our jobs at that time. After working for three years in the corporate environment, Victor received a promotion—with increased responsibilities—that he found challenging. After more than a year working in the foundation world, I was thriving in my job with enormous intellectual and interpersonal stimulation. I even joined a local Toastmasters Club to further develop and practice my public speaking skills and attended a monthly writers group. Victor and I bundled up and rode our mountain bikes every weekend throughout the winter months whenever the roads were not too icy or snow-covered to find a path wide enough to pedal through with our bike tires.

I saw no outward signs of Victor wrestling with his sexual identity issues at that time; we were connecting with each other and making our marriage work from my vantage point. I didn't pretend he was no longer struggling. But I was feeling cautiously optimistic and wanted to believe he was finding his own way to stay committed to our marriage.

With enough vacation time accumulated to consider traveling together, Victor suggested we drive our car— bringing along our bikes—to visit his parents who had recently retired and moved to Florida. We scheduled our trip for a week in March. We left early in the morning and drove straight through from New Jersey to Florida in about 16 hours.

Away from the cold and snow, we were bubbling with excitement to be in Florida for a tropical getaway. Victor's parents showered us with lots of delicious food and positive attention. We rode our bikes on the packed sand of Daytona Beach and on paved roads through the flatlands of the Everglades—we could pedal for miles and miles on the straightaway without any hills to climb. We played tennis, visited Walt Disney's Epcot theme park, and enjoyed his parents' swimming pool and the luxurious surroundings of their upscale, gated community. I believed we were "living in the moment"—too involved in enjoying the refreshing change of scenery to think about the fallout since last year on St. Patrick's Day.

One afternoon, Victor's parents started chatting about their real estate adventures in Florida; they were quite successful in buying and selling properties and had their eyes on yet another McMansion in the neighborhood.

"We did meet one real estate agent who introduced us to her adult son," said Victor's father. "A nice guy, well-dressed with good manners. But, son of a gun, we later found out the guy is gay. Can you believe it? A nice-looking, educated guy. And he's gay."

"Dad, we have friends who are gay," said Victor. "People can be gay and still be nice."

"But really, we feel sorry for his parents," said Victor's mother. "And what that poor woman has gone through being his mother, we just can't imagine."

"Did this guy seem happy?" I asked.

"Oh, yeah," said Victor's father. "He makes lots of money and wears a lot of expensive jewelry. But I just don't get it. Why does a guy like that have to be gay?"

"Good question," I said, taking advantage of an opportunity for solidarity with Victor by taking a stand against ignorance and intolerance. "I don't think anybody knows what makes people that way. Sexual orientation is a big mystery to me."

Victor remained silent.

~~~

Victor and I had many things to talk about on the long drive back home to New Jersey. We always had good times when traveling together. A road trip was always a good bonding experience. The only downside was we missed Champ, who was being cared for by a trusted pet sitter while we were away.

It was hard to believe Champ had been in our lives for over five years, ever since our friend Marty (our longtime friend from our college days who sang Victor's song at our wedding) showed up from Massachusetts with a puppy without a home. As usual, Marty descended upon us with a car full of people and his guitar for the weekend. But the puppy was a total surprise. He told us he had found homes for all the other puppies in the litter except this one. I think Marty knew exactly what he was doing when he showed up with that cute, little runt-of-the-litter puppy. No way would Victor let Marty take that puppy to the pound. Victor had such a big heart to take Champ in. He adored that dog, and she adored him. It was a jubilant scene when we arrived home. Champ seemed so glad to have us back home.

~~~

I decided to visit my mother in Vermont for Easter. I asked Victor if he wanted to come along but he said he could use some alone time. I thought nothing of it, given the fun we had just had in Florida.

Despite a rocky sendoff on the following Saturday morning—we awoke to find it snowing and Champ had a messy intestinal episode on our cream-colored carpet that needed to be cleaned up—I left for my trip up north as planned. Victor urged me to be careful and told me to call him when I reached my mother's house to let him know I was safe.

I did call him and left a message on the answering machine at 4:30 p.m. that I had arrived safely. I had made a point not to query him about any of his plans for the weekend. Usually I tried not to call him more than once a day when I was away to avoid generating any more anxiety in me than I already had. I also tried to convince myself that "checking in" with him was different from "checking up." I called again at 7:00 p.m. and 9:30 p.m.; no answer.

"Well, Victor must have a hot date tonight," my mother said when she heard that my phone calls didn't go through.

"That's really helpful," I replied sarcastically, although that was precisely my worst fear. "I think you read too many Harold Robbins books. Happily married men don't go around acting like playboys."

"But when the cat's away, the rat will play," she said.

"Victor's not like that," I said. "Actually, Victor has told me I never have to worry about him having an affair with another woman. He's my husband. I just have to trust him."

I had no idea why my mother made these comments that night. Did she sense my uneasiness? Was she trying to probe for more information about my anxieties and insecurities? Given her "all men are beasts" belief system, I knew it would only make matters worse to confide in her. Besides, I wanted to spare her from worrying about my marriage, too. So I said nothing more about it.

~~~

I called Victor at 10:00 a.m. on Easter Sunday to wish him "Happy Easter!" After receiving a busy signal the first attempt, I reached him on the second call.

"Hey, are you okay?"

He mumbled some words I could not decipher, yawning incessantly.

"You sound really out of it. I think I called at a bad time. I'll try to talk to you later."

Going through the motions of Easter, I found myself wrestling with "worst-case scenario" thinking, bracing myself for what I would go home to and finding out what Victor had done while I was away. Instead of pondering the meaning of Easter, I was reflecting on the top "Most Disturbing Statements" made by Victor in the past year: "Fidelity is no longer important"; "I have daily torture about my same-gender feelings for sexual bonding with a man"; "I have sacrificed acting on my desires because of you"; and "1991 will be the year we separate and I'll find a homosexual lover." I was sinking deeper into a pit of depression. I tried to visualize this pit had a trampoline at the bottom, allowing me to bounce back up to emotional equilibrium. Sometimes this visualization worked, sometimes it didn't.

Victor called me back, quite unexpectedly, at 6:00 p.m. to apologize for his morning yawning, but offered no explanation besides not having had his morning coffee.

~~~

When I returned home the next day, Victor lavished me with attention.

"Tell me all about your visit," he said.

I gave him a brief rundown and then ventured a casual inquiry to him, hoping he wouldn't say something troubling.

"Did you get to do anything fun this weekend?"

"No," he said without further explanation. "Hey, you seem to be a little down. Do you have a case of the blues?"

"I think you could say that. I've had an emotionally exhausting weekend."

"Well, I'm glad you're home. I'll pour you a glass of wine. It's time to relax."

Later that night we reconnected in a sexual way—a spontaneous decision. Even though I wanted to feel a physical connection to Victor, I was starting to question my sanity. How could I make love to a man who made me feel so insecure? Was it reasonable to trust him to respect our commitment to be honest about any actions that violate our marriage vows? Was I acting on blind faith or denial of real trouble? Or was I letting my imagination run away with me? That night I preferred the path of least resistance—slipping away from my resolve to make self-preservation my number one guiding principle and placing myself at risk for more heartbreak.

Chapter 10

My workplace was buzzing with activity in April. We had a new President at the Foundation with lots of energy and fresh ideas on the strategic direction of our work. For example, he called everyone back from their business travel to attend an urgent all-day staff retreat on a Saturday. The purpose of this retreat was to focus on how we could strategically increase the number and quality of the Foundation's grantmaking initiatives within the next year.

I still found it hard to believe I worked in a place that took the business of philanthropy so seriously. I had worked in other nonprofit organizations that sometimes struggled to cough up enough money to make the next payroll. And there we were, debating the pros and cons of accelerating our grantmaking. I was learning the process of giving away money in an intelligent way required a great deal of thought and consensus-building in this Foundation. *Oh, if only my grandfather*—an immigrant from Sweden who worked as a laborer in the marble quarries of Vermont when he was my age—*could see me now.* Furthermore, *I wish I could somehow share this experience with my father*—a skilled worker in a machine tool company until he died. They would be impressed I was working with dedicated people who really cared about making wise investments in programs and people with the Foundation's millions of dollars. I embrace the humbling wisdom of the Chinese proverb: "One generation plants the trees; another gets the shade."

Much to my surprise, I—along with a handful of other coworkers—received a special dinner invitation from the Foundation's President and his wife at their home on a Tuesday evening in April. This was one of the President's "get to know one another" initiatives on a personal level. I brushed up on my dinner party etiquette—yes, I actually checked out *Emily Post's Etiquette* book at the library to review the proper way to handle myself as a guest of a VIP—and did my best to blend in with the others in a relaxed manner. And I made an important exception to my vegetarian lifestyle: When a beautifully plated dish with chicken rollatini and broccoli was placed in front of me, I ate it—all of it. And every bite was delicious. It was the only occasion in five years of strict vegetarianism when I ate a cooked animal—and it was the last time I ever did. I know without a doubt it was the right thing for me to do because I didn't want to draw attention to my vegetarian preferences.

~~~

The following Sunday was the christening of the twin girls of Sally and Jacob, our longtime friends. Sally and Victor were close during their high school days as part of a group of fun-loving and sometimes wild teenagers in New Jersey; that friendship continued throughout college with frequent letter-writing exchanges between them. When Victor and I moved to New Jersey, Sally made sure to include us in her social life. We eventually met Jacob, rejoiced in their marriage, and visited each other frequently. We were thrilled when they had their first child, a girl, and were equally thrilled when Sally later gave birth to beautiful twin girls. Much to our surprise, Sally and Jacob asked Victor and me to serve as godparents for one of their twins. We joyfully accepted this honor and participated in the christening service at their local church.

Sally and Jacob were an interfaith couple—straddling the religious divide between one being Catholic and the other being Jewish with the superimposing belief that "God is Love" and love is greater than religious doctrines—but agreed to raise their girls in the Catholic faith. Victor, who was raised in the Catholic tradition, understood the responsibilities and symbolism of being named as godparents, and I was happy to go along with this plan. We had a reputation among our friends as being open-minded, tolerant, and respectful of the beliefs of others. In fact, we championed the plight of misfits and outcasts. Apparently, the priest wasn't too fussy about the current religious orientations of individual godparents, as long as we were willing to make a public commitment to participate in the nurturing of these precious children consistent with the Catholic faith.

"I think we were chosen as godparents because we're good at remembering everybody's birthdays, we show up when people invite us to their children's events, and we bring nice presents," said Victor.

"As long as we don't get in trouble with the Catholic Church for being who we are, which is far from saints," I replied. "Remember, it was your godmother—your father's sister—who made delicious homemade cheesecake for our engagement party, enough for 50 people. And her husband was our official photographer at our wedding. We need to take this godparent responsibility seriously."

"Sally knows who we are. I consider it an honor. We won't let them down."

"Yeah, but did you hear what Sally's father said after the church service? He said nowadays it's the responsibility of godparents to pay for the college education of their godchild."

"Oh, he's such a joker. Besides, who knows what will happen to all of us 18 years from now?"

"Just the same, we better do the best we can to be involved in this child's life. As the saying goes, 'it takes a village to raise a child.' So let's brush up on some children's Bible songs, along with the hand motions. For starters, there's 'This little light of mine, I'm gonna let it shine.'"

"'I've got the joy, joy, joy, joy, down in my heart,'" he sang with gusto.

"'Be careful, little eyes, what you see,'" I added.

"Oh," said Victor, "I never learned that one."

~~~

A week later, I was scheduled to take a business trip to San Antonio, Texas, to lead a workshop for some grantees—who manage the communications activities of volunteer caregiver programs—on developing effective newsletters, as part of a national interfaith conference.

The day before I left on my trip, I planned a three-hour bike ride with Victor on Saturday morning, a dry run of my presentation for feedback from Victor to bolster my confidence in the afternoon, and then an evening get-together with him and his work friends.

Victor decided to take me on a bike ride on scenic back roads. All was well until Victor pedaled out of sight ahead of me. *Not again*, I sighed to myself. *I'm really tired of togetherness activities that turn into solo activities.* I soon came to a fork in the road. I stopped in my tracks. My anger toward Victor started to percolate. *How can he be so thoughtless and rude? Is it too much effort to glance over his shoulder to see I'm close by?*

But this time I changed tactics. I resigned myself to wait right there to see if I was missed before attempting to backtrack. I waited about 20 minutes. Then I saw Victor, first as a speck in the distance, come barreling toward me.

"What's wrong with you?" he cried out. "Can't you figure out for yourself the right road to take?"

I glared at him, as I witnessed my once-chivalrous knight in shining armor go rogue.

"Put yourself in my place. Can't you see my dilemma? I see a fork in the road, with nothing but trees and open fields on both sides of each road. I don't know which way to go. So here I am, waiting for you to notice I'm not riding with you."

"Well, now I'm never going to hear the end of you having hurt feelings because you feel abandoned out here on the back roads. It's no fun for me when you can't keep up with me."

"Keep up with you? Isn't it an awful feeling not to know where I am and why I'm not riding with you? You take all the fun out of cycling together when you do this to me. Besides,

I'm the one who should be angry here. This happens over and over again. We're like a broken record: We have a conflict, you get mad at me, and then we never resolve the problem."

"Shall we call it quits on this bike ride today?"

"Absolutely not. I'm no quitter."

"You want to keep going on?"

"Only if you promise to be my guide, making sure I make the right turns and keeping me in sight."

"Okay, let's move on."

~~~

Later that afternoon when we returned home, Victor turned up the stereo real loud and started causing a ruckus playing with Champ.

"Listen, I need some peace and quiet now so I can concentrate on my workshop presentation," I scolded him.

"Oh, am I annoying you?"

"Frankly, yes. And remember you promised to listen to my dry run and give me some feedback. I need you to be supportive."

"Okay. Go ahead and do your thing. I'll sit here at the dining room table and listen."

I shuffled through my note cards, sat up straight, and recited my opening lines. I tried my best as I did a runthrough of my talking points.

When I reached the halfway point in my presentation, Victor insisted it was time for a break.

"Let's take a nap."

"A nap? In the middle of my workshop? Am I putting you to sleep? That's not very encouraging."

"Really, I'm so tired from the bike ride. I need a nap. I'll listen to the rest of your spiel later."

"Go ahead and take your nap. But I have to prepare for my trip now so I can spend the evening with you and your work friends like I promised."

Victor went upstairs, with Champ trailing behind, and took his nap.

Later, we spent the evening with Victor's work friends, caught up in our personas as a fun-loving, happily married couple.

~~~

I woke up early Sunday morning, with only two hours to capture some sense of connection with Victor before my departure for Texas. At breakfast, Victor announced his plans to wash both of our cars before I left for the airport.

"You want to spend our precious time together washing the cars? Can't you see I'm feeling out of sorts about our relationship?" I said, crumbling into tears.

"What's wrong now?"

"I don't feel like leaving for a trip when our relationship is not in a good place. I'm in trouble. Our marriage is in trouble. I'm constantly playing tug-of-war with my feelings and you at the same time."

"What can I do to help?" he asked.

"Can you just hold me for 10 minutes and help me pull myself together?"

"Of course, I can hold you. Everything's okay. I know you'll do a great job in Texas. I love you very much."

Victor had a way of restoring my sense of balance and perspective when my emotions were off kilter. He could be so tender with me, coaxing me to believe in myself and assuring me everything would turn out just fine.

~~~

Victor was right. My trip went smoothly. The conference was held at a retreat center, formerly a convent; the accommodations were sparse, but the people were warm and welcoming. My workshop participants seemed eager to embrace the content of my presentation; they asked engaging follow-up questions and wrote favorable comments on the evaluation forms I distributed.

Fortunately, I was able to compartmentalize my work life, keeping it separate from my personal life, on these business trips. But I needed a way to put the brakes on all the mind racing that kept me from falling asleep at night, whether I was at home or away from home. My Bible tells me that "The Lord is my rock, and my fortress, and my deliverer, my God, my rock, in whom I take refuge" (Psalm 18:2, RSV). Why was it so hard to put my trust in God to work things out?

I just have to toughen up and focus on being the strong woman I can be, I told myself. *I need to be my own sanctuary, finding that place within myself where I can feel safe and at peace.*

Chapter 11

As Victor and I approached our 13th wedding anniversary in June, Victor made a big announcement.

"I've decided it's time for me to finally take the big leap. No more pussyfooting around. I'm 35 years old. It's time to take action."

"What are you talking about, Victor?"

"Up until now, you've been the one who's taken the primary responsibility so we remain childfree. Now it's my turn. I think I'm ready to schedule my vasectomy."

"You are? That's marvelous news! You would go through this now? For us?"

"Yes. I've been thinking about it now and then over the years. And we've talked about it on and off. Other people have told us we'll change our minds and want children when we hit our 30s. But that hasn't happened."

"No, it hasn't. More than ever, I enjoy being childfree."

Victor and I often talked about how we have plenty of children in our lives, including nieces and nephews, a new godchild, and children of our friends. We had no interest in bringing a child into the world. We had worked with plenty of children over the years who didn't receive enough love and attention. We had no reason to change our strong commitment to being childfree.

"Everything I've read about having a vasectomy makes it seem straightforward. Snip, snip, by a doctor with a very steady hand, and it's done. And it means we will no longer have to use any birth control for the rest of our lives. It's one less thing to worry about as we move forward. I think it's the right thing to do."

"Oh, Victor. I think it's an incredibly loving thing for you to do. You must love me a whole lot to even consider this. I mean, I wholeheartedly believe that no man in the world loves his penis more than you do. And the fact that you would let a doctor come anywhere near your penis with sharp, surgical instruments takes a lot of courage and trust. You know I'll be there for you, every step of the way, to be supportive in any way I can be."

"Well, I hope I don't chicken out at the last moment. But I'm going to follow through on this. I'll call a urologist tomorrow to start the ball rolling."

"This is a wonderful anniversary gift," I said. I had read in etiquette books that lace is the theme for celebrating the 13th wedding anniversary. But Victor had sure topped that. I was grateful and so proud of him.

Victor did find a urologist who accepted his employer's health insurance and scheduled his procedure for mid-July. I was elated, reassured that *this is a good sign, right? Why would Victor go through all this if his intentions were to leave me and start a new life with a homosexual lover?*

In the meantime, we found ways to distract ourselves. I signed up for a weeklong class in Washington, DC, at the George Washington University, which my employer agreed to pay for. It was an intensive "crash course" on health policy; I wanted some formal classroom training on the world of policymakers, which includes government officials, elected politicians, and thought leaders concerned about the health and healthcare needs of Americans. I spent the week there in late June and learned a great deal.

When I returned home, we dashed off for a weekend trip with Zachary, one of Victor's friends and work colleagues, and his wife, Heather—a newlywed couple younger than ourselves. Also mountain bike enthusiasts, they invited us to tag along for a camping and biking trip in Massachusetts to explore the Cape Cod Rail Trail—a 22-mile paved bikeway that runs from Dennis to Wellfleet with campgrounds at

Nickerson State Park in Brewster. We had a blast together, cycling on flat terrain with scenic views of salt marshes, cranberry bogs, pine groves, and quaint villages. With lots of signage along the way and no forks in the road, it was impossible to become lost. Zachary set a good example for Victor, making sure to pace our cycling so that Heather and I were always in view—a togetherness adventure as a foursome.

"See, Victor, it can be done," I said. "An enjoyable bike ride without any drama."

"Come on, give me a break," said Victor. "This is a sightseeing trip, not an athletic event. We're barely working up a sweat. But still it's fun hanging out with these friends."

~~~

The day before Victor's vasectomy, I was scheduled for a one-on-one meeting with the Foundation's President. He met with each member of the professional staff, and it was my turn. With my growing awareness of the need to project myself more, I practiced good posture, making eye contact, and speaking out directly. He gave me positive feedback on my work performance and encouraged me to do more of the same. He also told me to be my own person, not always aligning myself with my boss and my department. I felt he was coaching me, and I appreciated his vote of confidence.

~~~

Out of respect for Victor's privacy, I didn't tell anyone except my therapist about his procedure until it was over. I drove him to his urologist's office and prayed for him as I sat in the waiting room. Afterward, he told me he appreciated my support; I felt we were back on track in taking care of each other. His recovery was swift. We both were relieved after his first successful urination and his first erection. He experienced some soreness for a couple of days, but not enough to warrant pain medication. After receiving final sperm count results a few months later, we could proudly declare, "Mission accomplished! Victor shoots blanks."

~~~

Even in the midst of these positive developments, I struggled to stay upbeat. I'm not ashamed to say I did care more about Victor than myself at this time because my love for him meant everything to me. *I'm on his side, no matter what,* I told myself. *We can face anything life throws our way as a united force.*

I was steadfast in my belief in the power of love. Love transforms people; life is no longer about me, me, me, but becomes all about us, us, us. Victor's joy is my joy; his pain is my pain. I reassured myself that we are not slaves to our feelings and emotions, which change from day to day. My willingness to put his wishes and needs before my own was consistent with my view that love is sacrificial, unending, selfless, and unconditional. I also believed when we care for others, freely give of ourselves to seek what's best for them, and then choose not to give up, our love grows. And my Bible told me, "love…endures all things" (I Corinthians 13:7, RSV).

Never for a moment did I doubt Victor's love for me during our years together before St. Patrick's Day 1990; I knew he adored me, and I adored him. It may sound corny, but I would wake up every morning and ask myself, "What can I do to make my husband happy today?" Likewise, he made me feel as if I was the center of his universe.

Looking back, I can see I had fused myself with Victor; my intense bond to him was my source of strength and meaning. I couldn't imagine my life without Victor; that's a failure of my imagination. And that means trouble. My notions of love were pure but incomplete, leaving little room left to keep myself out of harm's way. Yes, my unbalanced thinking led me astray.

Furthermore, I was learning in therapy about my lifelong patterns to minimize my own feelings and thoughts, deferring to others and trying to meet their expectations. It was too easy for me to retreat to my childhood mode of handling fear and uncertainty: withdrawal, isolation, and self-destructive eating. Living in a state of limbo—not knowing if Victor would stay true to me or abandon me—was stressful. Without a strong sense of self, I felt fragile and vulnerable. But I plodded on, hoping the power of positive thinking would overcome all my shortcomings and give me the confidence to deal with whatever happens in my marriage.

The issue of short-term medication use came up in therapy as an option to consider, which could bring me some relief. According to the *Diagnostic and Statistical Manual of Mental Disorders (DSM)*, I matched the description of dysthymia—"morbid anxiety and depression accompanied by obsession"—and medications were available to help manage my DSM code 300.4. But I wasn't ready to take this step without first exhausting all other options.

I set four personal goals for myself. I wanted to focus on ways to prevent episodes of deep depression; to develop a sense of empowerment about my work; to accept and express my feelings; and to feel good about myself.

I decided I could try harder to manage my feelings by developing my own set of behavior prescriptions, which I referred to as my fortress of safeguards to avoid episodes of deep depression. I would identify any triggers for depression early on, list all the feelings the trigger can generate, figure out my choices in confronting the trigger, and then choose the best option. I developed a list of 10 actions to ward off depression, which included listening to a relaxation tape, taking a bath, doing an exercise workout, talking to someone, and having a good cry. I also established a clear boundary: If I experienced more than three consecutive nights of sleeplessness (defined as less than four hours/night), I would take action to induce sleeping.

I believed in the power of my God-given mind to overcome any obstacle in my personal life. Knowledge of self was not enough; I needed to believe in myself and feel good about myself. I was motivated to build up my self-esteem muscles to become solid as rocks. I developed my own wellness statement—which served as a sort of mission statement and creed as my personal articles of faith—and recited this three-paragraph pledge to myself daily:

My Wellness Statement

I am a bright, capable, caring, attractive, normal-sized, congenial, highly motivated, and emotionally strong woman. I can express my full range of feelings in healthy ways and can speak up with confidence about what's on my mind.

I care deeply about my husband. I have a loving, supportive, and satisfying relationship with him. Although Victor continues to wrestle with his own issues (which have nothing to do with me), I remain committed to our marriage. I seek our continued growth as individuals and partners for as long as I can tolerate living with the ambiguities of his unresolved issues or he chooses to engage in activities that violate our understanding of fidelity.

I recognize the possibility that one day Victor may decide to act on his same-gender feelings. I choose to believe this is a possibility, not a probability. Regardless of the evolution of our marriage, I choose to make self-preservation my number one priority.

So help me God, I prayed.

Chapter 12

In September, Victor and I took a two-week vacation in the Pacific Northwest. Our itinerary was to take a plane to Portland, Oregon, where we lived during our first year of marriage. Leaving our bikes at home in New Jersey and instead bringing our camping equipment, we rented a car and planned to revisit familiar sites, as well as take a ferry ride to explore Victoria and Vancouver, British Columbia.

We started with a visit to our friend Sharon, who had worked with us when we served as houseparents in a group home for a dozen adolescent girls from troubled families. A dear friend, she had a doctorate in counseling and had started working as a dean of students at a university.

In 1978 when Victor and I were fresh out of college, we shared a burning desire to work with girls in a group home setting. We discovered many different organizations provided structured programs for boys—perhaps inspired by the story of Father Flanagan as depicted in the 1938 movie, *Boys Town*, starring Spencer Tracy and Mickey Rooney. However, precious few programs were dedicated to help girls. We wanted to make a difference and provide a safe and nurturing environment so these girls could overcome their childhood obstacles and traumas and achieve some measure of stability to survive and thrive during their teenage years. We found the perfect match for our pioneering interests when we landed a job as houseparents in a faith-based organization in Oregon. So we packed up all our possessions in our modern-day covered wagon—a brand-new, yellow Ford Fairmont we bought with the money we received as a wedding gift from Victor's parents—and drove cross-country, confident we were doing God's will.

Full of idealistic notions, we wanted to change the world for these girls. All of these girls had experienced significant abuse and neglect; some were the targets of incest (and their fathers were doing jail time for their behavior), and some had been runaways, escaping intolerable circumstances in their families. We considered this opportunity similar to a Peace Corps or missionary experience; low-pay work (room and board at no cost plus a stipend of $6,000 a year each) for a noble cause. We stayed on the job for a year and then returned to the East Coast to be closer to family and friends.

Sharon provided a warm welcome for us as we reminisced about our days as houseparents and inquired about the girls. We learned most of them made it through school and created new lives for themselves. A few of the girls completed the program but resorted to their street smarts to cope with addictions they developed. Some of the girls were lost to follow-up.

"How about the other couple who were houseparents before us? Any news on them?" Victor asked.

"Actually, it's a sad story," said Sharon. "After moving to upstate Washington to grow apples, they came on hard times. Life became complicated, and now they've split up."

"Split up? I can't believe it!" I said. "They were such a strong, born-again couple with such beautiful children. What happened?"

"Well, it turns out Arnold is gay. It was just too hard on Darlene and the children to all live under the same roof."

"I'm flabbergasted," I said. "I feel so bad for all of them. What in the world is happening these days? Latent homosexuals are coming out of the woodwork."

"We barely knew them, but I never sensed anything gay about Arnold when we lived here," said Victor. "I know he was rather burned out on the houseparent scene when we crossed paths. But he adored Darlene and their young children."

"My friendships with Darlene and Arnold have meant so much to me," said Sharon. "I try to stay in touch with both of them. It's so heartbreaking."

Victor and I stared at each other.

~~~

After leaving Sharon's home, we visited some of our favorite spots over the next few days. We spent an entire afternoon at Powell's Books—a book lover's paradise that occupies an entire city block—in downtown Portland. We hiked around Multnomah Falls and Larch Mountain, sunbathed in the "clothes optional" area on the Columbia Gorge, and tented our way through Washington State before venturing into the Canadian wonderlands of British Columbia. We had a wilderness experience on Mount Seymour and then enjoyed luxurious accommodations in a downtown Vancouver hotel. We were grateful for the simple pleasures of civilization such as easy access to food, water, and heat in a bear-free shelter, as well as sleeping on a mattress.

On the drive back to Portland, we stopped at the Elliot Bay Book Company in downtown Seattle. We studied the shelves of books, looking for treasures and marveling at the wide selection. We wanted to check out different parts of the bookstore so agreed to meet back at the cash register in 45 minutes.

When Victor spotted me later at our meeting place, he had a big grin on his face.

"I found something special for you," he said.

"A book?"

"Yes, a book. But I want to show it to you first before I buy it."

"Okay, show me the book."

Victor presented me with a paperback entitled *The Other Side of the Closet: The Coming-Out Crisis for Straight Spouses* by Amity Pierce Buxton, PhD. Published in 1991, this book "explores the major issues straight spouses confront when their partners declare their homosexuality or bisexuality and offers practical guidelines for resolving these conflicts in the direction of positive growth," according to the back cover.

"Shall I buy it for you?"

"Well, I guess so. I've never seen anything written on this subject."

"Neither have I. So let's get it."

"Wait—I'm not sure I want this book in our house." I paused. "I think it's kind of scary."

"Oh, come on. It's just a book. Let's give it a chance."

"Okay, you win. Buy the book. We can sneak it in and pack it with our camping equipment for the trip home."

"It's nothing to be ashamed of," he said. "And maybe you'll learn something useful."

"Aren't you going to look at this book, too?"

"Okay, I'll read it, too."

Victor did read the book after we returned to New Jersey. But I had a hard time even looking at the Table of Contents. So I took the book—concealed in a brown paper bag in my briefcase—to my therapist. He looked it over and told me it was up to me if I wanted to read it or not, and when. I decided I had other books I wanted to read first.

~~~

"I find this *Closet* book disturbing," said Victor, on a Thursday evening in October. "Virtually all the examples and stories are about people behaving badly before coming out to their spouse. So much betrayal, dishonesty, and anger over all the lies and deception."

"Oh? Are you ready to talk more about this now?" I said, looking up from my work papers.

"Well, yes."

"Have you had a 'coming-out' to me?"

"My coming-out was when I told you about my same-gender feelings on St. Patrick's Day."

" I'm certainly aware of the fact you're asking yourself questions about your same-gender feelings. But I've heard no word yet on any answers to those questions. Is it no longer a 'journey' for you?"

"Let's face it. I'm not 100 percent heterosexual."

"So what percentage are you?"

"I've told you before. I can't answer that."

"You know, if you're 96 percent or 98 percent heterosexual, I can probably live with that. But if it's a lot lower than that, I just don't know."

"It's not a math calculation or a probability word problem. It's the very core of my being."

"But you seem happy when we're together."

"Happy? I'm glad I don't have to keep my same-gender feelings a secret from you. But I want to make it perfectly clear: Our future is one of the many unknowns."

"Oh? What does that mean?"

"I love you very much, Vivian, and I have no intention of leaving you. At the same time, if I find myself in a situation where 'it feels right' to act on my same-gender feelings, I may do it."

"Have you already found yourself in situations with men in which there is a mutual sexual attraction?"

"Yes, I have."

"Do you understand acting on your same-gender feelings means losing me?"

"Yes, and I know we have an agreement. If I ever have sexual contact with someone else, I won't touch you in a sexual way without first telling you about it."

"Victor, I would want nothing to do with you after you've messed around with anyone else—male or female."

"Yeah, I know the rule, but I resent these boundaries. The leash from you isn't long enough."

"You feel like I have you on a leash?"

"Sometimes it feels like that."

His words made me feel so misunderstood. I had tried to be the opposite of a nagging wife, patiently giving him all the time and space he needed to come to terms with both his same-gender yearnings and his heavy drinking. But I had failed. I could see he felt trapped in our marriage.

"I sometimes feel that if you ever proposed the 'out of my life' option, I would resist, fight back, and persuade you to reconsider," I said, as I chose my words carefully. "But if I proposed the 'out of my life' option, you wouldn't put up any resistance; you would just let me go."

"No, that's not true."

I could see tears welling up in Victor's eyes.

It had occurred to me that the quantity and frequency of his alcohol use might be related to the intensity of his same-gender "daily torment" yearnings and his increasing restlessness about feeling trapped in our marriage. The more he drank, the more he tried to make his emotional pain go away. For him, binge drinking seemed to be an effective way in the short term to live in a state of inertia, refusing to make hard decisions about what to do. I wanted Victor to consider the impact of his drinking as a coping mechanism.

"Tell me, do you see any correlation between your same-gender feelings and your drinking?"

"No, I don't."

"Do you see any correlation between me and your drinking?"

"No, I don't. In fact, if you were out of my life, I would probably drink more."

"Do you see anything destructive about your drinking?"

"No, I don't. I only drink because I like to drink."

"Well, don't you think we've been living somewhat in denial about all these issues?"

"Yes, I do."

"Victor, maybe we need to talk more and figure out how to make things better."

"Yes, I think we do."

"How about me asking Dr. Barley if he's willing to meet with us as a couple to help us work on communicating and sorting out our feelings?"

"That's okay with me," said Victor, as he placed the *Closet* book on our bookshelf, next to my copy of William Styron's *Darkness Visible: A Memoir of Madness.*

Chapter 13

Dr. Barley agreed to meet with Victor and me for a couple of joint sessions, starting in October. During our first session together, Dr. Barley explored if and how we felt empathy for one another's pain and struggles. He also probed further for us to talk about each other's style of control, which prompted me to identify my preferred style as avoidance of confrontation—and anything else unpleasant or uncomfortable—and Victor's style as being a sadistic bully at times. Victor and I agreed that we both needed to work on identifying and expressing our feelings to one another, as well as healthier ways to handle our feelings. Most importantly, we needed to figure out what to do with our feelings after expressing them.

"Okay, I'll start by stating my feelings," I said, feeling emboldened in the safety of my therapist's office. "First, I love being married to Victor. He's my husband and the love of my life. But I also feel used, as if I'm a second-hand item and a stand-in. I feel vulnerable to being preempted, and I feel like I'm someone other than Victor's number one partner choice. I feel bitterness because Victor gives me such mixed messages, and life seems so unfair. I think his approach is that 'if nothing better comes along, Vivian will do.' I feel hurt. It's all so painful. I feel fear, and I feel threatened. And most of the time I feel so overwhelmed that I just want to die."

"I really do feel Vivian's pain," said Victor, making eye contact with Dr. Barley. "But I also feel anger. I feel torn between being true to myself and meeting her expectations. I feel trapped. Our future is structured as an ultimatum: If I act on my same-gender feelings, the marriage is over. But I also feel enormous love for Vivian. I want her in my life."

"Okay, now talk to each other, not me, when you express your feelings," said Dr. Barley.

So we did a do-over, speaking directly to each other. We also discussed our different views about fidelity that have evolved over time. Victor stated that having sex with someone else didn't mean less devotion to me, whereas I stated infidelity was totally unacceptable.

"How do you define your devotion to Vivian?" was Dr. Barley's follow-up question.

"For starters, it means unconditional love. No matter what, Vivian still remains my wife."

"I never said I'd stop loving you just because you become unfaithful. What I said was I would want nothing to do with you after you've messed around with anyone else. Our marriage is over the moment you have sex with someone else. Has that already happened?"

"No, it hasn't," declared Victor.

This session soon came to a close. Dr. Barley suggested we all meet again next month while I continue to meet with him on a weekly basis. He gave us an assignment for the next joint session: Jot down a few things that we consider hard to talk about with one another. I was glad we had met with Dr. Barley as a couple and considered it a productive conversation.

~~~

Naturally, I came in for our next session with a prioritized list of eight hard-to-talk-about items; Victor had one question for Dr. Barley, "What can be done when Vivian gets so bummed out?"

We did the best we could to clarify our issues as a couple. Dr. Barley encouraged us to work on being more spontaneous and less analytical about showing our feelings, as well as ridding ourselves of "guessing game" expectations and being more direct to one another in our conversations.

Later that night at home, Victor and I agreed it was time well spent to have met together with Dr. Barley for these two sessions.

"Dr. Barley is the very best at what he does, huh?" I said.

"Yeah, I'm glad you have an excellent therapist. Until now, I haven't really appreciated how serious and deep-seated your low self-esteem issues are. You really need help."

"Yes, I need help, but what about you?"

"Yeah, I'm holding my own."

"Well, we're still married, even though it feels like our marriage is hanging by a thread."

"As the folk singer Richard Thompson sings, I feel like I'm 'Walking On A Wire.'"

"Yes, I know that song."

"Let's just see what happens."

In the meantime, Victor and I had plenty of things to do—work commitments, social engagements, and family obligations, as well as holiday activities. And I decided to wait until after the holidays to look at *The Other Side of the Closet*.

~~~

In January of 1992, I breathed a sigh of relief: 1991 had come and gone, and somehow our marriage had survived another year. I decided to finally read the book Victor gave me.

You are not alone was the key message. According to its author—who discovered in 1983 that her husband was gay after 25 years of marriage—an estimated two million women and men in the United States are or have been married to a homosexual or bisexual partner. *Two million people have experienced this crisis in their marriages?* I found myself quibbling with the research methodology and math calculations—this estimate is equivalent to the entire population of Paris, France, or Philadelphia or twice the population of Rhode Island. Frankly, I didn't care about the precise prevalence numbers; I only cared about how I might fit the author's definition of "the straight spouse," which was unfamiliar and rather awkward terminology she used throughout the book—just the sound of this label made me cringe.

So now I'm the one who needs to take on a new identity as "the straight spouse"? I wondered. The label seemed so strange to me. I could understand its utility for sociologists in describing the phenomenon of couples in mixed-orientation marriages, as shorthand for women being married to men who turn out to be gay or bisexual and men being married to women who turn out to be gay or bisexual. But I didn't want this label imposed on me, reducing me to a one-dimensional artifact of the complex person I really am. Let's face it: How many little girls dream about how they want to grow up, fall in love, and become "the straight spouse" in their happily-ever-after marriage? None, in my opinion. That's not what I ever aspired to become. In fact, I've never even described myself as a spouse, a gender-neutral term I associate with insurance forms and legal documents. "Straight spouse" seems so impersonal, objective, and clinical—it's not the sort of term that creates a mental image or inspires empathy. I couldn't see myself embracing this label, allowing Victor's same-gender yearnings to define me in this way.

Most importantly, I was startled and moved by the dozens of heartbreaking stories about the men and women who were interviewed for this book—many with circumstances far more complicated than ours. The book described the impact of a partner's "coming-out" for the straight spouse in terms of "damage to the spouse's sexuality; destruction of the traditional marriage form; conflict of parental and spousal roles; crisis of self-identity; breakdown of trust and integrity; and disintegration of belief systems." I was appalled to read about how some couples had made alternative lifestyle "adjustments" to redefine their marriage in ways that accommodated the gay partner's sexual orientation.

I could certainly relate to the part about "disintegration of belief systems." I began to question everything I believed in: my marriage, my life principles, and my faith. What I found absent from this book was how the clergy were helping couples in trouble navigate these painful life decisions.

91

It seemed the very resource that many people, such as Victor and I, turned to for spiritual guidance and God's blessings for the wedding ceremony were clueless on how to help us with this unexpected crisis. But perhaps my expectations were too high: No religion has all the answers, and the clergy had full plates as shepherds of their flocks.

No way am I going to resort to any "alternative marital styles," I told myself, after reading descriptions ranging from having a sex-free marriage to tolerance for sex outside of marriage. While I had an open mind toward what arrangements worked for others, it was a no-brainer for me: exclusive fidelity in our marriage or no marriage at all. But most of all, reading this book made me sad, so very sad.

~~~

After dinner one night at home, I came up with the courage to talk to Victor about what I had been reading.

"I finished the book you gave me. But I didn't find any solutions."

"Did you learn anything new?"

"Well, I feel so sad about all the people with shattered lives who shared their personal stories, especially when children are involved. I guess revealing this hideous secret was the first step in coming to terms with their relationships."

"What do you mean by hideous secret?"

"You know, the whole 'coming-out' thing."

"Oh? That's what you call it now."

"It really shakes me up."

"How so?" said Victor.

"I've always thought about our sex lives as being truly wonderful, a celebration of our bodies and souls, an expression of the deep down, special kind of love we have for each other—complete with our own special kind of fireworks. But I've been thinking that maybe I've got this all wrong. Maybe what sex is all about for you is self-gratification. Maybe you're really just making love to yourself. I'm thinking that maybe my body is just some sort of convenient masturbation aid with moving parts. Maybe your yearnings to be sexually bonded with a man represent a yearning to be with more of a mirror image of yourself. Sex is not about us, it's about you. And I'm just something to be used, a receptacle for your sexual fluids."

"What a totally ridiculous and cruel thing to say," he said, as he glared at me. "I'm deeply insulted by your thinking. How dare you make such an accusation! If that's how you feel, you really don't know me at all."

"I'm just telling you what I'm thinking about. I'm trying to make some sense out of this monstrous situation. Okay, maybe I'm grasping at straws, but I really don't know what we can do and where we can go from here. My world has been turned upside down. This is not the way things are supposed to be. It's so unfair. It's a no-win situation," I blurted out in tears.

"I really don't want to talk about this anymore right now. This is outrageous. You have really gone off the deep end. I need a time-out to lick my wounds from your vicious attack on me."

Then he stormed out of the room.

Chapter 14

"Based on your work with me over the past two years, what is your clinical assessment of my risk for some kind of breakdown?" I asked Dr. Barley at our next session.

"If you let it, this can take you out," he said. "Based on your background and coping mechanisms, you can get yourself in real trouble. That's why we're spending time on unraveling your thinking patterns and focusing on your feelings."

"I know I have some rather twisted ideas."

"You are a highly functional person struggling with a great deal of fear-driven stress in your life, Vivian. I see you working so hard. So—let's back up and talk about what's going on with you now."

It was time to play hardball in therapy. I spoke about my fears and recent interactions with Victor, about feeling moody and on edge, as well as feeling like a crummy wife. And I was starting to feel I was the beast of burden in my marriage and doing all the heavy lifting, subservient to Victor's emotional needs to the exclusion of my own. Given Victor's episodes of unpredictable eruptions of anger and my reactionary resolve to calm things down at all costs, I felt qualified to write an autobiography entitled *Living in a Volcano*. Yet, Dr. Barley told me I was entitled to live a fear-free, pain-free, and shame-free life. I didn't have any inherent flaws in my personality, but I needed to change my fear-driven thought patterns. I continued to read dozens of books in my journey toward self-actualization, including *Prisoners of Childhood: The Drama of the Gifted Child and the Search for the True Self* by Alice Miller, PhD, and *Feelings: Our Vital Signs* by Willard Gaylin, MD.

~~~

On a Wednesday evening in June, Victor insisted we were reasonably intelligent and sophisticated adults who could sit down together and watch the PBS broadcast of a BBC production of *The Lost Language of Cranes*. He didn't tell me much about the movie, other than "it's not about those long-legged, long-necked birds." He did tell me a review in *The New York Times* mentioned this movie contained a homosexual coming-out as a plot element.

"Okay, I'll watch it with you. It's just a movie on TV. I'll give it a chance."

But it turned out to be a powerful movie that spoke directly to my fears. After 30 years of marriage, the main female character in the movie—a copyeditor—discovers the truth: First, her 20-something son announces he's gay, and then her husband reveals his gay sexual escapades during their marriage. This was a double whammy, a double dose of dealing with two coming-out experiences in her family at the same time.

I found the movie devastating, yet I kept my feelings to myself—too scared to start a conversation with Victor that might make things worse for me.

"Can you handle this movie okay?" asked Victor.

"I don't know. It's really painful to see this woman go through such emotional turmoil. A little too close to home, isn't it?"

"Only homophobic people would find this too uncomfortable to watch."

"No one in this household is homophobic. Champ is handling this just fine," I said, as I reached over to stroke her fur as she slept, curled up in a ball, next to me on the loveseat.

For Victor, the movie was all about the coming-out experiences of the two men. But for me, it was all about the woman, who tells her husband at one point: "Think of me for once...My life's like the punch line of some stupid joke." *That's exactly how it feels.*

The message of the movie became clear to me: Life was unfair for everyone involved. All the denial and deception caused unbearable pain. The situation seemed hopeless to me. Witnessing another woman go through a similar situation made my own feelings come to the surface.

I felt myself sinking lower and lower, consumed with a sense of utter hopelessness and concluding that my life was a hopeless mess and I was a hopeless mess.

I'm just not strong enough to survive this hard punch, I lamented. *I can force myself to become self-reliant, but what's the point? Whatever joy, sparkle, and zest for living I have comes from knowing someone cares about me and that I matter—regardless of my successes and failures—in an unconditional way.*

~~~

I started to lose interest in living; anticipatory anxiety with its multiple layers of what-will-happen-next? fear was as debilitating as the actual loss of my marriage. I transitioned from "I'm depressed" to "I hate myself for being depressed" to a state of numbness. I realized that when I feel this down, I have to turn off all my feelings and somehow let the mood pass.

Fortunately, Dr. Barley came to the rescue, as he coached me to express my feelings to others with nondebatable "I feel…" statements and reminded me I always have choices and options—even when all options may seem undesirable. He encouraged me to rank self-compassion higher than compassion for others.

"Where is the anger?" he asked me over and over.

I can say I had a million things on my mind, but anger wasn't one of them. You see, feeling angry terrifies me.

Without evidence to the contrary, I had figured out at an early age that anger makes any situation worse. Not only did I see, as a child, plenty of bloody fistfights instigated by bullies and neighborhood playmates who received beatings with a leather belt from their sadistic parents, but I witnessed, as a teenager, my best friend's father in a fit of rage throwing her down a flight of stairs when she came home past her curfew. Then there was the time when my mother, as a widow, came home with black and blue bruises, burn marks, and broken ribs caused by a man she loved; she told me she had said something that made him mad during a night of heavy drinking.

Words spoken in anger could have serious consequences, making my world spin out of control.

But it goes deeper than that. The intense discomfort I feel when I'm in the presence of an angry person is paralyzing; I fear things can get ugly real fast. My heart beats faster, my tension-filled body braces for attack, I hold my breath. I regard people as tornadoes when they're mad, with their menacing swirl of emotions destined to cause destruction, suffering, and pain. I dread unleashed anger; loud voices, strings of cursing obscenities, fists pounding on tables, and objects flung against walls unnerve me. With years of practice, I've learned to place constraints on any anger I feel. *Be slow to anger*—that's my motto. Anger means danger.

Victor knew about my aversion to anger; he would hardly ever see me angry. He would be the one to raise his voice, and I would be the one who tried to smooth things over. We had conflicts and disagreements but rarely let the situation escalate beyond rational discourse. No scenes in our home to rival the volatile relationship we saw in movies between the characters played by Elizabeth Taylor and Richard Burton in *Who's Afraid of Virginia Woolf?* or the vicious bitterness between Kathleen Turner and Michael Douglas in *The War of the Roses.*

As you can tell, I don't do anger well, which is a major understatement. So I've become a master at avoiding anger, casting it aside, hiding it, dismissing its utility, and rationalizing my way around it. I decided it's best for any anger to be displaced, out of sight, out of mind.

However, I did feel manipulated by Victor to be the one to tend to his issues. *Could it be Victor's goal is to increase my comfort level about dealing with his issues for him?* I needed to get a grip on myself and put things in perspective.

I put the brakes on further exposure to such upsetting movies and books; I didn't share Victor's interest in the coming-out stories of others. And I came to the conclusion that I'm *not* an all-loving, all-accepting, and all-tolerant person. I can only live with my own well-defined boundaries.

Yet, I chose to keep a final resolution at arm's length, letting it wear me down into the abyss of self-destructive thinking. This led to the return of my struggles with some demons from my past, namely, my relationship with food and my history of weight control behaviors via binging and purging. I was smart enough to come clean with Dr. Barley about these urges.

~~~

It was time to seek medical assessments about my health. I found a primary care doctor for a checkup; she treated me for an upper respiratory infection and ordered some laboratory testing. She also advised me to reduce my excessive caffeine intake and gave me a prescription for a low-dose sleeping aid to take at bedtime. After receiving the test results, she told me I had a hiatal hernia and referred me to a gastroenterologist for further evaluation, which resulted in me being told I have a medical condition called "rumination."

"Perfect," I said when Dr. Stewart, a gastroenterologist, gave me the news. "There's actually a medical condition that corresponds to the way I manage my personal life—going over things repeatedly in my mind, over and over again. I do so much mind racing. So what exactly does this rumination diagnosis mean?"

"This condition—where you regurgitate small amounts of food from the stomach, rechew it, and then either reswallow the food or spit it out—is similar to a cow chewing her cud," he said. "The good news is that you came to me with this condition. It's rather harmless when it doesn't happen frequently. But you need to be sure to eat small portions of food at one time and eat several small meals throughout the day, rather than large meals. That should keep things under control."

"And what about when I have a presentation to make or have some dental work done? It's really embarrassing for this to happen in public. Do I simply not eat before I have to speak in front of a group?"

"I'll give you a prescription to calm down your digestion for times like that. But the most important thing to know is this: Plenty of doctors would love to perform all sorts of unnecessary, costly, and invasive testing procedures on you. Your job is to keep these people from going that route. If your symptoms become worse, let me know. But, for now, I think you'll be fine."

I also made a visit to Dr. Kay Appleway, a nutritionist with a doctorate in chemistry who I had met while working with hospice years earlier. She provided valuable guidance on taking care of my nutritional needs as a vegetarian and suggested an individualized vitamin supplement regimen to promote wellness.

I started a new campaign to take care of my health, which included doing my best to eat well, sleep well, and exercise more, with almost daily workouts at the Foundation's new fitness center. I also started meeting with a Shiatsu massage therapist regularly, to help me learn how to relax my body and reduce my stress levels. These actions helped me avoid resorting to the destructive eating patterns of my past.

Throughout this period, I remained functional in my job. In fact, morale was high under the leadership of our Foundation's President, and the staff was geared up for great achievements. I was invited to be part of several groups to work on specific initiatives, including a major replication of a successful program that helped communities establish interfaith volunteer caregiver projects. My visibility among my colleagues was increased when I was selected as part of a team to give a presentation to the Foundation's Board of Trustees, making a strong case to move forward with this initiative. As a result, the Foundation directed more than $100 million to help start these caregiver projects in hundreds of communities across the nation, helping volunteers provide services to neighbors with chronic health conditions so they can remain in their communities and live independently.

I thanked God for the privilege of working in the foundation world! This Foundation was the greatest workplace I could ever imagine. The people were smart and committed and knew how to make important things happen. My dream job had exceeded my expectations. Not only did the Foundation provide the opportunity to further develop my knowledge and skills as a communications officer, but it served as my lifeline to a world beyond myself. It made no sense to me how I could be living in the best of times in my work life and in the worst of times in my personal life.

~~~

During this time Victor started to develop stronger one-on-one male friendships with colleagues from his workplace. Although he had a wide circle of friends, he began reaching out to guys in his office who were younger than he was. He seemed to cycle through these friendships, often inviting a friend over for the evening to talk, watch TV, and drink beers. Victor never did find a drinking buddy who could match his drinking habits, but he kept trying. He also started spending more time with Calvin, a friend from high school who worked as a dispatcher and driver for a limousine service; he was single and lived alone in an apartment about 30 miles away.

Victor always made sure I met his friends; they all came across to me as healthy, responsible, heterosexual guys. His friends sometimes kept him company when I was away on my one- to three-day business trips to Boston, Charleston, Dallas, Minneapolis, Philadelphia, Pittsburgh, San Francisco, and Washington, DC. I had a hunch he was showing his male friends excerpts from the gay porn video he had in the house, as a sort of litmus test to gauge any interest or disinterest in same-gender sexual activity. I would imagine him talking with his friends to detect if he could find any homophobic tendencies so he could taunt them unmercifully. I was curious if any mention of "tree climbing" came up in their conversations as an inside joke; I no longer enjoyed listening to my cassette tape recording of Carly Simon's *Boys in the Trees.*

~~~

In the fall, Victor approached me with an idea.

"Calvin has a couple days off from work and has asked me to come along with him to visit Stephanie in Nantucket."

Stephanie was a close friend of Victor's while they were in high school. She was in charge of our guest book at our wedding reception and gave us our Cuisinart as a wedding gift—an extravagant purchase that probably cost a week's paycheck at the time. She even came out to Oregon when we lived there to visit us. She introduced us to the music of Bruce Springsteen, way before most people started their day with Bruce Juice. I considered her my friend as well. I knew she had been working as a nurse at the hospital in Nantucket for a couple of years. But we rarely had contact with her except Christmas card exchanges.

"Oh? I would like to see Stephanie," I said. "It's been years since we all got together. I thought she kind of drifted away from her friends in New Jersey."

"Well, you know her. She has her ups and downs. And so does Calvin. But I know you're wrapped up in your work these days. I think Calvin wants this trip to be a guy thing."

"Are you asking my permission to go with Calvin? You know you can go wherever you want. Are you sure Calvin will be good company? He can be rather moody."

"I know he can be a pain sometimes. But it would be fun to see Stephanie and see what her life is like on the island."

"Don't you think she'll think it's strange I don't come along?"

"No, she knows you work. And she'll be working at the hospital some of the time while we're there."

"You won't be doing anything there that would upset me, would you?" I asked, daring to voice my insecurities about his plans.

"Of course not. It's just a brief visit. You know you can trust me. I'll be with Calvin, for Christ's sake. He's not gay."

"Well, then. Have fun, and be safe."

I wasn't going to stop Victor from making a visit to Stephanie. She was my friend, too. So was Calvin.

~~~

Victor and Calvin did make the trip without me. When Victor returned, he didn't have much to say to me.

"It was good to see Stephanie, but the people are kind of stuck-up there," he said, somewhat disappointed. "And Calvin wasn't that much fun. Both he and Stephanie gave me a hard time about my drinking."

"I'm glad you're back home, safe and sound," I said, relieved and affirmed that I wasn't the only one to notice Victor's overuse of alcohol.

But then Victor threw another curve ball my way.

"I've been thinking that it's time for us to start shopping around for a new house," he said. "If we put our townhome up for sale, I bet we can make a tidy profit and upgrade to a larger house with more property in a less congested part of New Jersey."

"You want to go house shopping together? Now? Why in the world would we spend time applying for a new mortgage and relocating when we don't even know what's going to happen to our marriage?"

"Perhaps this is exactly what our marriage needs. A new place to live. With more space. And closer to your workplace. A new chapter in our lives."

"I don't think it's a good idea at all," I said in a calm and quiet voice.

It seems Victor's the one grasping at straws now, I thought. *How can moving to a new house save our marriage from ending in ruins?*

"Does that mean you don't want to see what's out there?" he said. "I've been looking at the classified ads. I see some good deals out there."

"If that's the way you want to spend our precious time together on the weekends, looking at houses for sale, you know I'll come along. But don't expect me to be enthusiastic about this idea. Moving is the last thing I want to do."

"Well, let's give it a chance. You never know what we'll find. And I'll begin fixing up our place, starting with painting the family room, so we can put up a 'For Sale' sign. Let's just see what the possibilities are."

This doesn't feel good to me, I thought.

Chapter 15

Victor did make good on his plans to tackle a wide range of home improvement projects, using death-defying tactics to paint the high ceilings of the family room and stairwell, removing stains in the carpet, and reseeding our weed-ridden lawn. In October, he posted a "For Sale by Owner" sign in front of our home. We never knew when someone might ring the doorbell to look over the place so we made sure the house was always in showcase condition.

We also started looking at homes for sale, weighing the pros and cons of each real estate opportunity. I was a good sport and went along with Victor's house shopping excursions. We made a low bid on one house, contingent on the sale of our home; but the homeowner rejected our offer. Actually, Victor's improvements and our extensive clean-up attention to our low-maintenance townhome made us better appreciate what a nice home we already had. Victor eventually decided we would postpone further house shopping adventures until after the holidays.

~~~

In the midst of competing priorities, I received a work assignment on short notice to attend a celebration in Philadelphia.

The day of the event was dark and dreary; in the late afternoon I took the train to Philadelphia and then a cab to the address. The mood was festive, with many city officials and about 100 mental health consumers gathered. I was introduced to the crowd as a representative from the Foundation, requiring me to stand up for recognition without any expectations that I would make remarks. I mingled and listened to stories about this organization's positive impact on the community. I was fostering goodwill to drive home the point that the Foundation not only provides funding for this work but also cares about staying connected to the people who are doing the work and those being served. Confident that I had stayed long enough at the event after others made their formal remarks, I decided to make a gracious exit. Night was descending, and I wanted to return home as early as possible in such bad weather. I asked the event coordinator about how to hail a cab in this part of the city; she told me she would make a telephone call to a local cab company and directed me to wait inside the main entrance for the cab. I waited 20 minutes; no cab. I requested follow-up on the cab ride and was told it may take more time, due to the heavy rain.

"It sounds like you need a ride," said a tall, middle-aged man who I had briefly met in the big room where the open house was held.

"I'm all set and waiting for a cab," I responded.

"Well, you know, this is a not-so-good section of the city. A cab may or may not want to show up here."

"Oh? I had no trouble with a cab bringing me here this afternoon."

"Nighttime is different," he said, as he walked over closer to me and lowered the volume of his voice. "Listen, I'm an undercover police officer. I know what I'm talking about. I'm always glad I pack a gun when I come to this part of Philly." Then he patted the slight bulge on his side under the left arm of his sports coat, which I assumed indicated he had a shoulder holster.

"The rain is really coming down now. I'm sure that's why the cab is delayed," I said optimistically.

"Where do you need to go?"

"I need a ride to the 30th Street train station."

"My car is just a block away. I can give you a ride there."

"That's very nice of you," I responded diplomatically, even though I was somewhat suspicious of his motives. "But I think I should wait for the cab."

"Do what you like. But there's a good chance that cab will never show up."

"Oh?"

"I can understand you feeling awkward taking a ride from a stranger," the man said. "Here's my card."

I took the business card he handed to me and glanced at its contents, which looked like something printed up at a local Kinko's without any official-looking logo. I wondered why he didn't just flash a badge at me, the way I'd seen on TV.

"I'm hesitating because I really don't want to make a scene here. I want to get home safely as soon as possible."

"Trust me," he said. "I'll take care of you all right."

I looked out the window; the rain was relentless. I decided to take a chance, hoping for the best.

"Okay, let's go," I said. "Thanks."

I walked with him in the rain to his rather beat-up car and slid into the passenger's seat, with one hand clutching my briefcase and the other hand gripping the door handle. Then it occurred to me: *Hey, this may be a gift. If this stranger intends to cause me bodily harm, it's my way out of my personal problems. If I'm as depressed as I think I am, I should just let go and let tragedy happen. With me out of the picture, Victor can start his new life, with a nice chunk of change from my life insurance payout.*

I kept up a steady stream of chatter as we rode along unfamiliar streets, not knowing if we were headed in the right direction. Within 15 minutes, he stopped the car and let me out in front of the train station in the pouring rain.

"See, you can trust me."

"Thank you very much for the ride," I said as I climbed out of the car.

When I arrived home later that evening, I told Victor about the incident.

"I was really foolish and really lucky that I didn't end up raped, mutilated, and dead in a back alley tonight," I said.

Victor seemed untroubled.

"What's wrong with me?" I added. "Don't you think it's alarming I would take a ride in a car from a total stranger with a gun?"

"Hey, nothing happened after all," said Victor in a nonchalant manner. "No big deal. It was nasty weather out there tonight."

It made me upset that Victor dismissed the entire drama of my evening. Could it be he didn't really care what could have happened to me? Or was it easy for him to chock it up to what he considered was my overactive imagination?

The next day I asked my secretary to verify the information on the business card the stranger gave me. She made some calls and then reported the telephone number was out of service. So I sent a handwritten thank-you note on Foundation letterhead to the address on the card, hoping it would not come back marked "Return to Sender." It never did.

~~~

A few days later, I stopped after work for my scheduled appointment with Irene for my Shiatsu massage. She worked out of her home, located on the last lot of an unpaved, dead-end road. I parked my car in the driveway behind her car. This was my fifth visit with her so I was familiar with the layout of her front walk and groped my way in the dark through the hedges leading to her door.

As I rounded the corner past the clump of bushes at the end of the walkway, I froze. The front door was gone, the windows were smashed, and, straining my eyes in the darkness, I could see a large, gaping hole where the roof over the living room once was. Charred rubble was everywhere. Only the detached garage in front of the house stood intact. I stepped around to the back door to discover the remains of the kitchen, nothing but a charcoal shell.

I took a deep breath and then let out a long sigh. The house was desolate, a total loss. It was easy to imagine no survivors. Whatever had happened to Irene and her children, their car was left behind. Forcing myself to think clearly, I scribbled a note—"Dear Irene, What a nightmare! How can I help?" with my first name and telephone number—on a piece of scrap paper I found in my backpack and placed the note under the windshield wipers of Irene's car.

Quite shaken, I drove straight home and dialed the telephone numbers of local fire stations, police departments, and hospitals, searching for any information about Irene. It felt like a conspiracy: "No information can be released to those other than immediate family members," echoed each switchboard operator.

Finally, I received a telephone call from one of Irene's neighbors who found my note on Irene's car. She told me Irene was in pretty bad shape in the hospital's burn unit. Her hair went up in flames, her face was now disfigured, and both her hands—those precious healing hands that brought pain relief to so many people—were severely burned. Her children were unharmed, but Irene's recovery was uncertain. I felt terrible for Irene, but I also felt so self-centered to realize that meant no more Shiatsu massage stress reduction sessions for me; I was on my own to figure out how to learn to relax my tension-filled body.

~~~

Later that week, I was lying in bed sleeping, with Champ at my side, when I heard a noise that startled me. I opened my eyes and saw Victor, naked and standing still with his back toward me over on the far side of our master bedroom by the door to the hallway.

"Victor, are you okay?" I asked, as I raised my head and squinted to see him in the darkness of the room.

No response.

I rose up to walk closer to him. He was in a daze, urinating a full stream in the corner of our carpeted bedroom.

Was he sleepwalking? I thought. Victor had no history of sleepwalking but there he was, apparently oblivious to what he was doing. I didn't want to make things worse so I just watched him as he finished the task at hand and quietly slipped back into our bed, wrapping himself up in our comforter.

I waited a few minutes and then nudged him.

"Victor? Victor, wake up. Are you okay? Do you know what you just did?"

He started to stir.

"What's wrong? Why are you bothering me?" said Victor.

"You need to see what you just did."

"I'm too tired. Leave me alone. Tell me in the morning."

"It is morning, and you just peed on our rug."

"Oh?"

"Yes, I just want to make sure you're okay."

"I'm okay."

"Well, that's good. I'll leave you alone. I'll let you clean it up in the morning, or else you won't believe me."

~~~

The next morning, Victor did scrub the carpet clean, puzzled by the entire incident but not too concerned about it either.

"What was that all about?" I asked.

"I don't know."

"Should you see a doctor?"

"Maybe, but I'm embarrassed. Let's just forget about it."

"I watched you. I think you thought you were in the bathroom."

"Well, the whole thing was strange. Maybe I had too much to drink last night before I went to bed. I think the carpet will be okay."

"I don't care about the carpet. I care about you."

I was scared and worried about Victor's behavior.

"I'm okay," he said. "Really."

"Okay. I'll try to lighten up. But, you know, Champ is confused now. You don't set a good example for her when she sees you doing what we train her not to do."

"Very funny. I'm sorry. I don't think it'll happen again."

~~~

109

When I met with Dr. Barley for my next session, I described myself as a human shock absorber. Unlike Victor's nonchalant reactions, Dr. Barley found my experiences of the last week quite disturbing, especially the thoughts that accompanied my decision to accept a ride from a stranger with a gun. After extensive conversation, he came to a firm conclusion: It was time for me to start taking an antidepressant. I agreed with him and complied. He arranged for me to see a psychiatrist, Dr. Sylvia Beacon, for a second opinion, who started me on a new low-dose antidepressant right away—its effects would kick in just in time for the holidays.

Chapter 16

Within 10 days I had found a friend in Zoloft, which offered some degree of relief from my state of depression. Far from being a "happy pill," it took the edge off my teetering moods of darkness; I didn't have to work so hard to achieve a steady emotional state. *Maybe there is some truth behind all this talk about treating chemical imbalances*, I thought. *Such a tiny orange pill was now waging war against my Jericho walls of tension, which just might come tumbling down in this great test of faith in the power of an antidepressant.*

The best part was this medication didn't interfere with my ability to think clearly and work productively. I was no longer resistant to using it as a tool for dealing with my despair; I knew I needed all the help I could get. I was confident my therapist would be able to work with me more effectively as I moved forward; my medication would serve as training wheels as I learned how to keep my balance through the ups and downs of my personal life.

~~~

Much to my surprise, Victor made a visit to a new physician recommended by his psychiatrist, Dr. Boland, who he continued to visit on a monthly basis. His new doctor had apparently dismissed the urination incident as "nothing to worry about" since it only happened once.

"So does he want you to do anything about it?" I asked after Victor came home from work later that night and told me about his visit.

"He wants to do some routine testing on me next week. It's something called a sigmoidoscopy, which helps him check for any polyps by inserting some flexible tubing through my anus."

"What does that have to do with urination? I know enough about your anatomy to understand that's an entirely different orifice, isn't it?"

"Hey, I'm not the doctor."

I paused and then blurted out a question without my usual editorial filter to be sure I was emotionally prepared to handle the answer.

"Victor, have you been shoving foreign objects in your rear end?"

"No, nothing foreign. Only things made in America or from people who speak English."

I was both annoyed and amused by his response.

"Very funny, Victor. I'm trying to be serious here. Did you tell him about your Prozac and your daily use of alcohol?"

"When he took my medical history, I said I had two drinks a day. I also told him I was taking Prozac. He made no comment about that."

"Dr. Barley explained to me that Prozac increases serotonin levels in the brain to promote mental balance whereas alcohol decreases serotonin. So it's counterproductive to combine the two. When one of his patients is on Prozac, having even one beer is an issue because it robs the person of some of Prozac's benefits."

"Well, it's a good thing I'm not one of Dr. Barley's patients."

I felt bewildered by the lack of attention the doctors were giving to Victor's issues. It was hard to believe they really cared at all about him. Or perhaps Victor was not forthcoming with them either?

"I don't know why other people don't pick up on the serious needs and issues you have. Is this the best the medical community can do for you? I'm so frustrated. You deserve the very best medical and mental health attention. But this is what you get."

"I know you think I have a drinking problem."

"Well, is it true that the thought of going through a 24-hour period without a drink would be very uncomfortable for you?"

"The only drinking problem I have is that I don't drink enough," he said, as he paced around the kitchen. "That reminds me: I need to take a trip to the liquor store for more supplies tonight."

Once again, Victor saw no connection between his drinking and my worries about his well-being. He went shopping and came back with a bottle of Drambuie for me, even though I thought I made it clear I wasn't going to do anything, such as drink alcohol, to compromise the benefits of my antidepressant.

~~~

Two weeks later I had my first follow-up appointment with Dr. Beacon so she could check on how my antidepressant was working out. She complimented me on my looks and told me I was an accurate historian; I guessed that meant she had checked in with Dr. Barley, with my permission, to compare her notes on me.

I did tell her I was feeling tired, rundown, and worn out, as if I really couldn't deal with anything emotionally complicated. I had crashed early the night before, sleeping from 7:30 p.m. to 6:30 a.m. without a bedtime sleeping aid. I considered this to be "escape sleep," not restful sleep, because I really didn't want to deal with being awake. She came up with a good word for how I felt—scattered—and made an adjustment in my medication.

~~~

A work group leader at the Foundation gave me a major editing assignment with an unavoidable time crunch that required heavy editing to condense the viewpoints of 10 strong personalities; I knew it was impossible to satisfy them all. My immediate supervisor, Katarina, was also dealing with a huge workload.

In the midst of this work, my Vice President of Communications, Jack Briggs, popped his head in my office with a newsflash.

"It's official now. I just met with our Foundation's President, who has approved raises for our entire department."

"That's great news, Jack. I appreciate the raise. Thank you very much."

"However, he made a comment about you. He said you were a better worker in 1991 than in 1992."

"What? But that's not true," I said.

"I was surprised to hear his comment, too."

"When I met with him last summer for our annual one-on-one chat, nothing like this was said to me. What measures does he use to come to this conclusion?"

"I don't know. All I can say is I like the work you've done for me."

"Should I talk with him about this misunderstanding?"

"No, I don't think that's a good idea now. We're having our company holiday party in a couple of days. No more formal meetings until after the holidays."

"What can I do to make things right?"

"Talk to Katarina about this. She may have some ideas. The Foundation is going through some internal changes now. I'm not certain what's in store for all of us in the coming year, including me."

"I will talk to Katarina. I'll do whatever it takes to work this out."

"Hang in there, Vivian. We can only do the best we can."

~~~

When I came home and told Victor about my conversation with Jack, he was unconditionally supportive.

"That's outrageous. You work your tail off. What does Katarina say about this?"

"I hope I can talk with her tomorrow. She's working incredibly hard these days. I really don't want to be a burden to her, exposing my anxieties and self-doubt about all this."

"Every organization has some degree of game-playing and internal political dynamics," he said. "It sounds like this is someone's idea of cracking the whip to maximize productivity. I see it every day in my workplace. And, of course, I bet your friend in Human Resources will be the last one to hear about any of this, if at all."

"And you know I'm clueless about playing games with people. I'm the worker bee who gets the work done, not the mover and shaker who wants the spotlight. Plenty of other people can take the glory."

"Well, I think you're the greatest. And I'm confident Katarina will come up with something to help you feel better about all this. She knows all the players on the chessboard and what it takes to come up with a winning strategy."

"That reminds me of the Chinese proverb I once found in my fortune cookie: 'Life is like a game of chess, changing with each move.'"

"As the Cowardly Lion in *The Wizard of Oz* would say, 'Ain't it the truth, ain't it the truth,'" said Victor, as he started to mimic the antics of this beloved movie character who had a desperate need for courage.

~~~

The next morning I finished my rush assignment— shaving down 31 pages to a more organized and reader-friendly document of 10 pages—and handed it off to the leader of my work group. Then I was able to cross paths with Katarina, who was also working on a tight deadline to complete a project.

"Do you have a couple of minutes for me before you leave for the day?" I asked.

"Yes, come in my office now," she said, as she motioned to close the door behind me.

"Did you hear what Jack told me yesterday about the President's comment on my work this year?"

"Yes, Jack told me about it."

"Can you believe it? I don't know how to handle this. It upsets me so much for anyone to be disappointed with me, let alone our President. What do you think I can do about it?"

"Well, my sense is that other things are brewing around here on a higher level," she said, as she lowered her voice. "And I'm not sure why people are picking on you. You're a tremendous help to me, but I'm guessing your work isn't visible in a compelling way to others."

"You know I'm willing to take whatever corrective action is needed to make things right."

"I know you are conscientious in your work. But I guess we need to figure out ways to increase your visibility. Perhaps one step is to speak out at large groups when our Foundation President is in the room."

"I can step out of my comfort zone to be more outspoken in front of others. I'm low on the totem pole around here. By definition, I'm a behind-the-scenes worker; I listen and learn from others. But I can work harder to make a concise comment or offer an intelligent insight when it seems relevant—without coming across as being obnoxious."

"Another suggestion is to focus on improving your writing skills."

"I certainly can do that. After all, I'm learning from the best—you! Everyone comes to you to make their documents more coherent and polished. In fact, more and more I see so many demands on you from the top. I want to become a more skilled writer to help lighten the load. I thought it was enough to aspire to become a Katarina Junior, supporting you in every way I can. But I see I need to do more than that now."

"So those are two areas to focus on for now. And I'll put in a good word about you to others whenever I can."

"Thank you, Katarina. I'll try my best. Let me get out of your way now so you can meet your deadline."

~~~

With a plan of action to deal with the latest workplace development, I coached myself to transition into a festive, yuletide mode. Victor received a welcomed bonus at his job, which he used to buy a large, state-of-the-art television set that I nicknamed "the monster TV." Victor and I had many holiday commitments to be with family, friends, and work colleagues. We were on our best behavior when attending our company holiday parties. Victor was outgoing and full of charm, helping me make a positive impression at the Foundation's party—I wore an elegant party dress I bought for the occasion, and we made a special point to interact with the Foundation's President and his wife.

We hosted our traditional New Year's Day Open House, which spilled over into a birthday celebration for Victor who turned 37 years old in early January 1993. I then took a two-day business trip to Fort Lauderdale, Florida, to attend a conference.

Victor and I were getting along just fine during this time; we were a united front in facing the challenges of the new year together. Or so I thought.

In mid-January, I arrived home from work before Victor did. Champ was glad to see me and followed behind as I made my rounds—taking Champ out to the back yard to relieve herself, turning up the thermostat for the heat to come on, and going upstairs to change out of my Alcott and Andrews corporate attire.

I pushed the "Play Messages" button on the answering machine as I started to change my clothes and heard an unfamiliar male voice after the beep.

Victor, this is Brewster. I'm returning your call about the room for rent.

It's available now. Call me back as soon as possible and let me know what day you want to move in.

I dropped down on my knees next to our bed in front of the answering machine. *Wrong number?* I thought. I pressed the button to hear the message again. For a split second I considered erasing it or just pretending I never heard it. But then I faced the facts. The message was left for Victor. The telephone number was a local exchange. Could it be Victor was looking for a room for rent? Did he give this person our home number, not his work number, as a callback number? Or could this be someone playing a cruel joke on me?

I couldn't believe Victor was forsaking me. Perhaps the congenial way we were relating to each other over the holidays was only the calm before the storm. After all the drama and heartache over the past three years, had things really come to this point? I took a deep breath and tried to steady my nerves. Could this be the cowardly way Victor came up with to break the news that he's leaving me and our marriage behind?

Chapter 17

Twenty minutes after I had first listened to the voice message, Champ started barking at the sound of Victor's car backing up in our driveway. She scrambled down the stairs to meet him at the front door, while I made my way downstairs in slow motion.

"Hey, Champers, I'm home." Victor reached out with both hands to grab her as she jumped up in his arms. "You are such a smart dog. I'm glad to see you, too. Where's your tennis ball? Go fetch your ball," he commanded as he released her to go on a search mission.

"You beat me home for a change," he said, as he turned and greeted me with a kiss. "And how are you?"

"Not so good," I mumbled.

"More drama at work today?"

"Work was okay. Coming home wasn't okay."

"What are you talking about?"

"You have a message on our answering machine."

"Who called?"

"Someone named Brewster wants you to call back as soon as you can. He says he has a room for rent that you're interested in."

"Oh, man. He called here and left a message?"

"Yes, he did. What's going on?"

"Come and sit down so we can talk about this," he said, as he motioned to sit on the couch. "I don't have a speech prepared or anything. Give me a few minutes to collect my thoughts."

"I'm not interested in hearing a speech. I want to know what this is all about."

"Well, you're not going to like this. But I've made a decision. It's time for me to be on my own and find out who I really am. So I've been checking around. I made some calls about rooms to rent from the classified ads. I'm getting ready to move out."

"In other words, you're getting ready to dump me and throw away our marriage? And when were you planning to tell me about your decision to ruin my life?"

"I know this is a hard blow for you. It's not easy for me either."

"But you promised me you would never leave me. And I believed you," I said, as I broke into tears. My feelings of anger were crowded out by the sting of rejection and my terror at the thought of being alone.

"Yes, I did say that. But things change. People change. I'm truly sorry."

"Well, I refuse to turn this into a big emotional scene," I said, as I forced myself to regain my composure. I was able to switch gears by letting my crisis intervention training kick in, focusing on Victor and some concrete details to help normalize a situation that was far from normal. "First of all, let's be practical. A room for rent doesn't make any sense for you. I just can't picture you as a boarder in some rundown rathole of a rooming house, with kitchen privileges if you're lucky. You can do better than that. How about an apartment?"

"I'm trying to keep the cost down. It's not going to be cheap living on my own."

"I'm sure you can find an apartment you can afford not too far away from work."

"Maybe you're right about that. An apartment, huh?"

"I know it's a step backwards. Remember all the shabby apartments we've lived in? But you can make the best of it. The most important thing is to live in a safe neighborhood—without the landlord living underneath, if possible."

"Ah, yes. I remember those days."

"And what about Champ?"

"Oh, I wasn't planning to bring Champ with me."

"Ditching me is one thing, but how can you leave without Champ? You two are so close. She's your dog. She adores you. Wrong gender, huh? You're discarding her, too?"

"I think Champ will only get in the way."

"Well, I love Champ. I would never abandon her. She has a forever home with me if you don't want her. And what about me? What happens to me now?"

"You'll stay here."

"Is this the part where I'm supposed to beg you with all my heart to stay? Or do I just let you go and then fall apart?"

"We both have some time to get used to the idea. I haven't even found a place yet. But you know it's the right thing for me to do. I just hope you won't hate me forever. I still want you in my life. I just need to find out what life is like on the other side."

"On the other side? It could be hell."

"Yeah, I know. But that's the way it is. I'm stepping out to the other side."

"Victor, I love you and want what's best for you. But, you know, there's no such thing as a trial separation. Once you leave, there's no turning back. We're done. Our marriage is over. And I'm really scared."

"I know. I'm scared, too."

~~~

The next day I called my therapist to tell him about Victor's plans, and I assured him I would be okay until our next session. Dr. Barley suggested we increase our time together to two sessions a week so we worked it out to meet on Mondays and Fridays. I knew this was a good idea; someone needed to keep close tabs on me. I was feeling fragile, as if an emotional riptide could pull me under to drown.

Within a week, Victor had found an apartment and packed up his things. Victor's friend Zachary had a pickup truck and agreed to help him move out on the last Sunday in January.

~~~

Victor and I discussed how we could work things out in a civilized way. First, we agreed to pay off the $20,000 loan his parents had given us as the down payment on our townhome. Next, because this was Victor's story, not mine, I insisted he would be the one to tell his family and all our friends about his move. I had no interest in sharing Victor's coming-out story with anyone. And I told him if anyone calls our house looking for him, I would respond, "He's not here now. Try his work number."

"And I've been thinking," said Victor. "Let's have dinner together every Thursday night. I'll come over here."

I decided this was Victor's way of showing me he didn't want me to feel totally abandoned; at least one evening a week I wouldn't be all alone.

"Okay, we'll meet for dinner on Thursdays until you act on your same-gender feelings, which you still claim hasn't happened yet."

"That way we can keep in touch. You know I care about you so much."

"It's hard to believe this is really happening. It's not a matter of you packing up your stuff for a camping trip."

"That reminds me: I want to take some of our camping equipment."

"That's fine with me. Champ and I don't have any tenting plans for the near future. I can't imagine sleeping in a tent without you." And then, realizing my future plans with Victor were gone forever, I broke into tears.

~~~

The night before Victor moved out was somber and bittersweet. Without any discussion, we made love one last time. I believed I would never again have sexual relations with anyone; no man in his right mind would want me, a bundle of damaged goods with emotional scars from my marriage with Victor.

~~~

Late Sunday morning, Zachary showed up with his truck.

"Vivian, I'm so sorry to hear about all this," he said. "So is Heather. We can't believe it."

"It's really awful, but don't worry. You aren't walking into a big scene here today. I'm no drama queen. And thanks for being a friend to Victor today. He needs all the friends he can get now."

"I'm only taking a few pieces of furniture I really need— the new stereo, the wood table my father gave us so I can use it as my kitchen table, a couple of chairs, and the bed in the guest room," said Victor. "I'll leave the other stereo for you. And I made some cassette tapes for you from the records I'm taking with me."

I felt no trace of concern at that moment about the fate of our shared possessions. Victor's absence would be such a monumental change that everything else seemed insignificant.

I couldn't bear watching Victor's departure so I excused myself for the afternoon and reminded Victor to watch out for Champ so she doesn't get underfoot when moving things out. Victor promised to call me the following day.

"And I'll see you on Thursday night," he said.

I took a long look at Victor to see if he showed any sign of changing his mind. He seemed focused on his packing details and ready to move on.

"Please take care of yourself," said Victor, as he wrapped his arms around me and gave me a lingering hug before we both let go.

"You're the one who needs to please take care of yourself."

I felt scared for Victor; he had more at stake than me. He was venturing out into the total unknown whereas I was left behind, preferably to hide out from others as I wrestle with my emotional upheaval.

~~~

123

I returned home after 6:30 p.m. with a new colorful outfit I bought at the mall to lift my spirits—I was determined not to come back empty-handed—and saw no cars in the driveway. I unlocked the front door and found Champ; Victor had left her free to roam the house, not our usual habit to confine her upstairs in the guest room when we're out. She jumped up and down, eager to greet me. Feeling numb, I walked through the house; it was so quiet. Even though most of the furniture was still here, it felt like a cavern, hollow and empty.

"It's just you and me, Champ, living here in the discard pile," I said, as I held her in my arms. "Victor's gone, and we're on our own now."

Chapter 18

I tried my best to pull myself together for work, which provided a respite from my newfound misery of living alone. During my commute, I would hum along with Nat King Cole's recording of the Jerome Kern tune to "pick myself up, dust myself off, and start all over again." But when that didn't work, I resorted to turning up the volume full blast to hear Linda Ronstadt sing *Cry Like a Rainstorm, Howl Like the Wind.*

I went through the motions of living my life, with the support of Dr. Barley, one step at a time. I also checked in with Dr. Beacon every two weeks.

I felt as if I were a piece of ragged driftwood moving along in a slow current, no longer tossed about in a raging storm. I tried to keep everything as normal as possible. Only late at night, when my mind racing was at high speed, did I feel completely overwhelmed.

Victor did show up on Thursday evenings for dinner and chatted about how he was navigating his journey "to be true to himself." He said he was exploring the world of classified ads in the local newspapers as a way to break into the gay scene. He told me about meeting one man, a waiter in an upscale restaurant where we had lunch together a few times. The waiter took Victor to his house after work. While they were talking and having drinks in one room, the man's homosexual lover was in the room next door, in bed seriously ill with AIDS.

"Are you crazy? He introduced you to his male lover?"

"Yeah, I thought it was a sweet gesture on his part."

"I hope you ran like a bat out of hell straight out the door."

"No, not right away. But it was a bummer. I decided not to stay much longer."

"Victor, you just stared AIDS in the face. If that doesn't convince you that you're playing with fire, nothing I say will make a difference. I'm really worried about you."

As sad as I was for myself, I was also truly concerned for Victor. My love for him was not something I could extinguish like a fire out of control. I was terrified about what might happen to him.

"Aw, come on," he said. "I'm not going to do anything stupid."

"You already have done something stupid. You left me."

"Oh, well, perhaps."

"Well, I guess nothing happened sexually if you're here for dinner with me tonight."

"I know that's our agreement. I'm taking my time to check out my options. Promiscuous behavior is not exactly my cup of tea."

"You can't consider me a confidant to chat about your gay scene escapades. That's just plain cruel. Can't you see how upset I am with all this? You already broke my heart when you left me. And now you're killing me with stories about your so-called adventures."

"Okay, I won't talk about it anymore. Are you doing okay?"

"I'm not doing well at all. This is a crash and burn for me. I used to feel like a somebody when we were together. Now I feel like a nobody, a nothing. And I don't know how to stop loving you."

"It's hard for me, too. But it'll get better as time marches on."

"Easy for you to say. Champ and I are doing our best to tough it out."

~~~

On Sunday morning, February 14th, Victor showed up at the front door and rang the doorbell.

126

"Happy Valentine's Day," said Victor, after I opened the door. "I brought you a gift."

He had a small, white rabbit in his hands and stretched out his arms to present this creature.

"A pet rabbit? You're giving me a rabbit? What a precious bunny. Let me hold it."

"Can I come in? I have a cage for the rabbit and can set things up. How about the kitchen? The flooring is bunny-friendly there."

"Yes, you can. But what makes you think I can take care of a rabbit when I can barely take care of myself and Champ?"

"You can do it. I know how much you love rabbits. You deserve a rabbit."

"What's all this about, Victor?"

"Well, I thought a rabbit would help soften the blow. I guess I won't be coming over for dinner on Thursdays anymore."

"Oh, so that's what happened." My spirits deflated when I realized this token rabbit was meant to be a transitional object to help break my attachment to Victor. "So you acted on your same-gender feelings. Our marriage is irreparably over. I'm history."

"Do you want to hear about it?"

"No. You can keep all the gory details to yourself."

"Well, I met someone special. He's a little older than me. But he's good to me. He's gentle. I think he's the one for me."

"Okay, that's enough. And I never want to meet him."

"Well, his name is Howard Fletcher. He's a well-respected professional and has an important job as a big shot in a nonprofit organization."

"Okay, you can go now. You can leave the rabbit here, though. I think I'll name it Clover."

"I'll give you a call later this week," said Victor as he shut the door behind him with a jolt.

I sobbed my way up the stairs to the master bedroom. *Do I still call it the master bedroom?* I thought. *It's just a room with an empty bed with clean sheets now.* I took off my wedding band and placed it out of sight in the farthest corner of my jewelry box. I recited to myself what Victor had told me on our wedding day and every anniversary celebration: *This ring I give, in token and pledge, of my constant faith and abiding love.* Now it was just a symbol of another broken promise.

~~~

Up until this point, I really didn't talk about my shattered marriage to anyone except Dr. Barley—and hardly anyone noticed. I continued using the word "us" in all my conversations because "we" and "us" flowed much more naturally than "I" and "me." But I decided I could no longer avoid the need to confide in a few people. So I called my mother in Vermont later that night.

"Mother, this is Vivian. I'm calling with bad news."

"Oh? What's wrong?"

"Victor has moved out, and our marriage is over."

"What? I don't understand what you're saying."

"Victor has moved out, and our marriage is over."

"Oh honestly. How on earth can this happen? What's the matter with him?"

"It's a real shocker. Are you sitting down?"

"Yes, I am. Tell me what happened."

"Victor doesn't want to be with me anymore. He wants to be with a man."

"A man? Not another woman?"

"That's right. Victor broke my heart, and I'm a mess."

"I don't understand this at all. What did you do?"

"I didn't do anything wrong. It's all about him."

"Maybe he'll come to his senses."

"That's exactly what happened. He came to his senses, and I'm out of his life now."

"Oh, no. This is horrible."

"I don't feel like talking about it anymore right now. I have a therapist who will help me. So don't worry. I just wanted to let you know."

"Does anyone else know?"

"Not really. I'm sure I can count on you to tell the rest of the family."

"How dare he hurt you like this! After all you've been through together. And he dragged you to that godforsaken land of New Jersey to live. Men are beasts, you know. I've told you that for years."

"Okay, I don't want to hear any lectures. I need to get some sleep."

I had no interest in hearing anyone trash Victor. It was a complicated situation. I had mixed feelings about him and our marriage. I didn't have the energy to try to make her understand the depth of my feelings of rejection. I wasn't looking for words of comfort from her; such words didn't exist. I only wanted to let her know what had happened.

"Why don't you come home when you can?" she said. "And call me back when you want to talk more. You know I'm a listening ear."

"I love you, Mother. Sorry for the sad news."

"Okay, goodbye."

~~~

The next day at work I found Katarina alone in her office and asked if I could speak with her. She invited me to sit down in a chair in front of her desk.

"I think you should know what's going on in my personal life. But I want to assure you I'll do my best to make sure it doesn't interfere with my job."

"Go ahead," said Katarina.

I was nervous about saying the words out loud, even though I had rehearsed them in advance to myself. "Victor and I are no longer together. He moved out."

"What happened?"

"It's a long story, but I'll give you the short version. Victor thinks he's gay, not heterosexual. He claims he never acted on his same-gender feelings when we were together, but he wants to find out who he really is. Of course, that means our marriage is over."

"How painful this must be for you," she said, moving from behind her desk to wrap her arm around my shoulder.

"I'm okay. Really. If anything, this means I'll have more time and energy for my work."

"Right now I'm concerned about you, not the work."

"Well, even though Victor is the one with the identity crisis, I'm the one who was catapulted into therapy. I'm still trying to absorb the shock of it all. Frankly, I'm worried about Victor. I don't think he has a strong support system without me."

"You know, lots of people have gone through difficult times in their marriages. I can name several people you know who have had a first marriage."

"Really? I don't know many couples who have gone through a divorce. And I certainly don't know of any couples who have split up because of sexual orientation issues."

"It happens. Please take care of yourself."

"You bet I will. I am woman, hear me roar, and all that. But I do feel rather fragile; my feelings are raw. So that's why I'm telling you. I need to tell my secretary because it's unavoidable I'll be receiving phone calls at work about all this in the near future. And I know how news like this spreads through the grapevine here."

"Yes, but when things like this happen, we need to support one another."

"I'll figure out how to get through this," I said, as I sat up straight in my chair. "No pity parties allowed. And I'm under the care of an excellent therapist."

"I'm glad you told me about this. Pace yourself, and be kind to yourself."

"Okay. Thanks for being so understanding. It means a lot to me."

I felt a sense of relief after confiding in her. And I did decide to keep a low profile in the workplace, sharing my personal news with only a few colleagues when it seemed appropriate to do so.

~~~

The news of our breakup spread rapidly as a chain reaction; Victor must have telephoned everyone. I screened every call and only picked up when I felt strong enough to talk about it.

When the call came in from my mother-in-law's number, I grabbed the phone.

"Hello, this is Vivian."

"This is Marion. I can't believe it. Are you okay?"

"Oh, Mrs. Locatelli. I guess that means Victor has told you about what's happening with us."

"Both his father and I are so upset. He told us he thinks he's gay and he moved into an apartment."

"Yes, that's true."

I was glad to hear her voice and grateful that Victor had found the courage to tell his parents about our situation.

"What a nightmare," she said.

"It seems like a really awful made-for-television movie, a soap opera that no one would want to watch."

"Victor is such a fool. You're the best thing that ever happened to him."

"But he's your son. He needs you to be accepting and understanding of him."

"But how are you?"

"I'm heartbroken."

"Of course, you're heartbroken. But you're the most wonderful daughter-in-law."

"Well, you've always been so good to me. You welcomed me into the family with open arms from the very start. I can't even think about no longer being part of your family."

"Well, that's ridiculous. We love you. You'll always be part of our family for as long as you want to be. Here, your father-in-law wants to talk with you."

"Vivian? What the hell is this all about? We're worried sick about you. We don't understand this at all. Victor has us so upset. Marion is just sick about this."

"I know it's difficult for all of us."

"We're planning a trip to New Jersey soon so we can get to the bottom of this. We can't do much here in Florida. We'll see you then."

"Sure. You can stay here. Oh, I don't have a bed in the guest room now, but you can stay in the master bedroom. Or I'll come over to wherever you stay, as long as Victor doesn't show up with a new friend."

"We're not ready for that. It's going to take a long time for us to sort things out."

"We all need some time. I'll talk to you soon."

"We love you, Vivian. See you soon."

I felt sad for Victor's parents. They were so proud of Victor and me and the life we had made together. I was sure this was a shock, something they never saw coming. I knew coming to terms with the circumstances of our breakup was hard for everyone involved.

~~~

Dr. Barley pointed out that taking care of myself included contacting a lawyer sooner, not later. I located a lawyer and scheduled an appointment to meet with her. After learning that divorce lawyers charge by the hour in 10-minute increments, I became motivated to script out my questions in advance and talk fast, without any long-winded monologues. The sooner the legal details were settled, the better it would be for all involved.

Chapter 19

I soon discovered how inept I was at making adjustments in my personal life. My first self-destructive reaction after Victor moved out was to stop eating. I simply had no interest in food. The Foundation's Food Service provided breakfast and lunch for all employees in the workplace; I typically ate a bagel with peanut butter for breakfast, a large salad with dressing at lunch, and many cups of black coffee throughout the day. On the weekends, I ate a bowl of cooked oatmeal or some yogurt. That was enough; I had no appetite. I made sure I had plenty of dog and rabbit food in the house so Champ and Clover were fed. But I just didn't feel like feeding myself so I didn't.

~~~

I embraced any opportunity for work-related travel. Over the next few weeks I served as a judge in Washington, DC, as part of an awards program for communications work in the foundation world; attended a conference on generalist physicians in St. Petersburg, Florida; and led a workshop with a colleague on best practices in communications for grantees in San Antonio, Texas. I was grateful to become so preoccupied with my job.

Victor called me every week. One Sunday evening he asked me to help him carry a new purchase, a futon he bought at Fortunoff, from his car to his upstairs apartment.

"What's a futon?" I asked.

"It's a couch that can be flattened to use as a bed."

"No one else can help you with this?"

"No one else is available. Besides, you can see my apartment."

I followed his directions and found his place. I helped him with his futon. He gave me a tour of his apartment, located on the second floor of a Cape Cod–style house. We walked through his small kitchen and living room with wooden floors. Everything looked clean and neat. I took a glance in the direction of his bedroom and bathroom, but kept my distance.

"So this is your new life," I said, as a clasped my hands together. "Your place looks nice. Are you happy?"

"I'm okay. How about you?"

"I could use a hug. I still miss you. I hate living alone. Thank God I have my job. That's my anchor now, as well as my work with Dr. Barley."

"Want a drink?" asked Victor.

"No, I'm not staying long," I said. I felt too awkward to be in this unfamiliar place; I had seen enough of Victor's new living space. "I'm going home now."

"Thanks for helping me with the futon," said Victor as he gave me a bear hug and walked me to my car parked on his street.

~~~

Victor and I met a few times at our townhome to discuss paperwork from my lawyer about drafting details for our financial agreement, as well as gathering information for our income tax filing. As we were discussing property settlement issues, I noticed Victor's hands.

"You're wearing a new ring now?" I asked.

"Oh, yes. Howard gave me his ring."

"What's with the globs of bright red yarn wrapped around it? That's what a teenager does when she wears her boyfriend's class ring in high school. So you're going steady now?"

"I guess so," Victor said with a sheepish grin. "His fingers are much bigger than mine."

"Oh, please. That's more than I want to know."

I had no interest in any intimate details about Victor's lover. Too much information can be a curse, in my opinion.

We learned all kinds of legal terminology: Our townhome had a new name, "the marital home." All of our belongings were called "marital assets." We cancelled all joint credit cards and bank accounts, as well as figured out how to come up with "an equitable distribution of property." It was easy to make such decisions because we had minimal debts and few prized possessions. We had a short-lived tussle over the baby grand piano; Victor wanted it but had no room for it in his apartment whereas I insisted the piano was my safety net if I became desperate for cash flow and needed to sell it to cover mortgage payments for a few months. Victor relented and let me keep the piano.

Of critical importance to me was being absolved of any financial liabilities relating to Victor after he moved out. *God only knew what sort of trouble he could find himself in or the sort of new characters in his life*, I reasoned. I also wanted to create an incentive for Victor to file for divorce as soon as possible (an 18-month waiting period was in effect at that time); I was concerned that he would just "never get around" to filing a divorce petition. His employer provided legal services as an employee benefit so I wanted no mention of sexual orientation issues in the paperwork to protect Victor from any potential discrimination issues in his workplace.

The solution proposed by my lawyer: I would buy out Victor's equity interest in the marital home by making affordable annual payments to him over five years without interest, with the initial payment due upon entry of the final Judgment of Divorce by the court. Victor agreed to these terms, although he had yet to secure a lawyer to represent his interests.

~~~

On the surface, I was taking all the necessary legal steps to move forward in dissolving our marriage. But the emotional undercurrent was taking its toll. Much to my surprise, I started losing weight—lots of weight. At five foot ten, I wore long, pleated skirts and long-sleeved blouses with long jackets at work. My clothes had become quite loose and roomy; when I put a belt around my waist, I had to punch holes through the leather to create a tighter setting for latching on my belt buckle.

During the winter months I wore several layers of clothing to keep warm, which also helped cover up my weight loss. After each heavy snowfall, I shoveled the snow out of the driveway, often alongside my next-door neighbor Lydia, a senior citizen who had been widowed for several years; she was stronger and more steady on her feet than me. My toes developed a mild case of frost-bite during one storm, which may or may not have been related to my rapid weight loss. A visit to a podiatrist resulted in a fitting for orthotic shoe inserts to correct the deformities of my toes, as well as wearing a special strap-on surgical shoe on one foot for six weeks; this enabled me to qualify for special boarding when traveling by airplane.

~~~

Later in March I learned about a friend of a friend whose husband was a university researcher with a specialty in sexuality issues. Upon my request, he agreed to meet with Victor and me to offer his opinion on how Victor was handling the changes in his life. I went along with Victor for moral support; it turns out I really didn't need to be there. This sexuality expert spoke with Victor while I was told to stay in the waiting room. After about an hour, I was called in to join them for a brief conversation. This expert said he was satisfied with his conversation with Victor, affirming him for the direction his life was taking. Then he took a long look at me, from head and toe, and said, "It looks like you could stand to put on a few pounds." So Victor had the blessings of a sexuality research expert, which provided some level of relief as I continued to worry about him, and I had an expert's permission to eat a couple of candy bars.

~~~

By April, my weight loss had become significant. I never tried to hide my weight loss, but I also didn't draw any attention to it. I was grateful I hadn't experienced a serious weight gain, a far more likely reaction given my food binging patterns as a teenager; I could easily picture myself dealing with the stress and anxiety in my life by putting on another 80 pounds and becoming a couch potato.

I started to develop a morbid curiosity in how my body was changing into something quite foreign and alien. I could feel my bones jutting out; the cushions of fat I was used to carrying around were deflated. My skin began to sag. I no longer felt strong; my muscles were starting to weaken, even though I continued my almost daily 30-minute workouts in the Foundation's fitness center.

I was unable to break the habit of self-deprivation; my image in the mirror was a tangible reflection of the emptiness and despair I felt. Although functional on the surface, I was on a downward spiral. Dr. Beacon added another medication to my regimen called Elavil, which is used for treating depression, anxiety disorders, and eating disorders; a common side effect is weight gain.

～～～

One night I stopped off to pick up dog food at the grocery store on my way home from work. As I rounded the bend of the dog food aisle inside the store, I saw Victor. He was with a man. They were wheeling a shopping cart together. They were beaming.

I had a sudden urge to vomit.

It was too late to hide. Victor made eye contact and approached me.

"Hey, Vivian. What a surprise to run into you here." Victor kissed me on my cheek.

"Champ needs more Mighty Dog. Is this where you do your food shopping now?"

"Well, let me introduce you to Howard." Victor turned to present a man taller than himself with blond hair, a flushed face, and a red nose, which made me think he was a heavy drinker. I felt too overwhelmed to engage in a polite exchange of words.

"No, this is awkward. I really can't handle this. I have to get out of here now."

I rushed out of the store without any dog food and ran to my car. *I will never go to this store again,* I vowed. My entire body shook; I took a few deep breaths and tried to calm myself down. *Is that what this is all about?* I pondered. *Victor traded me in for that?* I started to freak out, overwhelmed with competing emotions: anger, jealousy, sadness, disgust. Dealing with this whole situation had become so much harder now; I could conjure up images of the two of them to ruminate about. Such images became toxic, unbearable.

~~~

During my next medication check-in visit with Dr. Beacon, I told her about running into Victor and his new friend.

"There they were, right there in front of my eyes," I explained. "I could hardly stand it. I had told Victor many times I never wanted to meet that man. Oh…he has a name. Howard Fletcher."

"Howard Fletcher, you say? I know the man. He used to work in Human Resources in a place I worked. He's a big troublemaker. He ruins people's lives. I hate that man!"

"Really? What should I tell Victor to warn him?"

"Don't get me started on Howard Fletcher. He's one of the most despicable people on this planet."

"Oh, no. Now I'm really scared for Victor."

"Well, you need to focus on yourself, not Victor. Are you taking your medication?"

"Yes, I am," I replied.

"I think that's enough for today. Our session is over."

I left Dr. Beacon's office more upset than when I arrived there. I could see the mere mention of Howard Fletcher's name was a trigger for uncontrollable rage for her, so much so that she didn't even attempt to mask her feelings in front of me. I knew I had just witnessed something unprofessional that shouldn't happen: a psychiatrist showing intense emotions toward someone else in the presence of a troubled patient. *What kind of monster is this Howard Fletcher?* I thought. *What am I supposed to do now?*

Chapter 20

When I reached the inner sanctum of Dr. Barley's office later that day, I burst into tears as I sat in the familiar soft-cushioned chair where I could safely release my pent-up emotions.

"I'm okay. Really," I managed to sputter in between sobs. "Just give me a few moments to get a grip."

"Take all the time you need, Vivian," said Dr. Barley, as he reached over and handed me a box of tissues. "I'm not going anywhere. Whatever it is, we'll work it out together. I know you had an appointment with Dr. Beacon this morning."

"Well, that's the problem. It didn't go so well with her."

I told him what had happened.

"I don't want anything more to do with her," I blurted out. "Am I allowed to fire my psychiatrist?"

"You certainly are. What she did was inappropriate and unprofessional. I will take care of this myself. You never have to see her or have any contact with her."

"Really? That would be such a relief. I just don't feel comfortable with her now. She became so enraged at the mention of Howard Fletcher. It was scary for me. And now I'm really scared for Victor."

"I'm concerned about you, not Victor. You need all the support it takes to see you through this difficult time. I will talk to your primary care doctor as soon as possible about your medication needs."

"I feel better already. I guess I really can't do anything about Victor, right? Whatever he does is out of my control.

It's so hard to let go. I want the very best for him, even though I'm out of the picture."

"I know you care about Victor. But you really have to care more about yourself than him right now."

"I guess I have to accept the fact that Victor made his own bed, and now has to sleep in it, as the saying goes. I need to let sleeping dogs lie, huh?"

"That's a good idea."

~~~

I made several feeble efforts to reconnect with friends, trying to move beyond my natural inclinations for withdrawal and social isolation. I soon realized how difficult it was for others to relate to me without Victor; Victor was a point of reference in all my interactions with our couple friends. Perhaps these friends needed time to process what had happened between Victor and me; they may have felt duped as well, never thinking our marriage was in trouble. Maybe spending time with me was a reminder of how life can go terribly wrong even when everything on the surface seems quite the opposite. Victor was always the one who provided comic relief, as a sort of tonic in the humdrum of daily struggles to lift the spirits of others. But I—alone, in my current fragile state—was a reminder that life can be more toxic than tonic. I tried to joke that "sexual orientation isn't contagious," but it just wasn't funny.

Despite the awkwardness of my situation, I soldiered on, trying to make others feel comfortable being with me, focusing on what was new in the lives of these friends' children. For example, I was delighted when Sally invited me to come along with the twins and their older sister to visit the Rabbit Hole—an Eastertime tradition at a local gift shop designed for children to find their way through a maze of displays in the nooks and crannies of an old house that ended with a slide. That was far more enjoyable than trying to strike up meaningful conversations with adults.

I also tagged along for a few "Ladies Night Out" activities when friends invited me. I was a good sport but failed to see the fun in being with a table full of women; they seemed overjoyed to be away from their men and children for the evening and relished the latest gossip, which made me suspect I was the target of their hushed voices when my back was turned. *It's going to take a drastic change in thinking for me to consider a night out with a bunch of women as something fun to do*, I thought.

I could see myself morphing into the once-happily-married-turned-spinster mode; I preferred becoming playmates with their children than building a new identity as their woman friend going through a divorce. I made it clear it was okay with me if they continued to be friends with Victor; in fact, I had no problem being part of a gathering where he was invited. However, if he showed up with his new partner at any event, I would make a quick exit. They told me they understood.

The same dynamics applied to my interactions with Victor's extended family. People still invited me to family gatherings; I was the default guest when Victor decided not to show up at any event. That was fine with me; I enjoyed hanging out with my nieces and nephews and attending various parties, activities, and school events. I still was clueless on how to explain why it was always "Aunt Vee Vee" alone, not "Aunt Vee Vee and Uncle Victor."

"But it's more fun when both of you come to visit," my 10-year-old niece confessed, despite her parents' explanation about Uncle Victor no longer living in the same house as Aunt Vee Vee.

How do I tell a 10-year-old girl who I adore that I'm no longer her aunt and she's no longer my niece? I wasn't ready to break off ties with everyone I loved, just because Victor had a new life.

~~~

Alice, my former neighbor, showed up at my front door one day with a loaf of banana bread and an invitation to attend church with her, her husband, and their teenage son on Palm Sunday. I accepted both the bread and the invitation; perhaps it was time to see how a United Methodist Church would welcome a woman in divorce purgatory. I had stopped going to the church where Pastor Norman was the minister, too embarrassed and ashamed about how my marriage had turned into a failure. Going to church with Alice and her family was a positive experience; people were nice to me. And I convinced myself that if Alice cared enough to bake banana bread for me, I needed to care enough about myself to actually eat it. It took a whole week to do it but I forced myself to eat every crumb of it. *Behold this small victory*, I told myself.

~~~

My sister Claire, who was living on Cape Cod, Massachusetts, with her husband and teenage son, also reached out to me. She came to visit me during Easter weekend, and we spent the weekend talking and talking and talking. My big sister, 13 years older than me, had always been a role model for me; she was outgoing, a world traveler, and an excellent first-grade schoolteacher. She always told me to "be the best person you can be." I went to the same college that Claire did. I always looked up to her and admired the way she lived her life; she had charm, style, and a great sense of fashion. And she knew about men; she had dated lots of men until she married her husband when she was 30 years old. She also had firsthand experience in heartbreak when her college sweetheart broke up with her. Fortunately, our father was alive to help her pick up the pieces.

We went to New York City for the day on Saturday; she brought me to David's Pot Belly Stove on Christopher Street for lunch. She arranged for one of her friends in the city—someone who had been married to a man who turned out to be gay—to join us. It was helpful to meet this woman who had gone through a similar yet quite different experience, although

I was concentrating on the hard work of eating the piece of quiche I ordered, forkful by forkful.

We also stopped at a store with dresses on sale; a bright blue dress with white lace caught my eye. Claire encouraged me to try it on.

"Do they have this in size 14?" I asked.

"Here's a size 14, but I think you should try on a smaller size."

Claire was right. I ended up buying the dress in the size that actually fit me: size 6.

"Well, I can't believe I would ever fit in a size 6 dress. The sizing must really be off these days."

"How long has it been since you bought new clothes?" asked Claire.

"Oh, not since Victor moved out. I know I've lost some weight, but something must be wrong with the way these dresses were made. Even size 6 isn't a tight fit."

"The dress looks great on you. I'm glad you found something you like."

~~~

When we came back to my house, I tried the dress on again in my bedroom.

"I have a really strange favor to ask you, Claire," I dared to ask. "No one has seen me naked since January when Victor moved out. Would you be willing to take a look at my body and tell me what you see?"

"Of course, I will."

I took off my clothes and slowly twirled around.

"So what do you think?" I asked, as I looked to see what Claire's face would reveal. I saw her pause and take in a big gulp of air before she spoke.

"Vivian, you're very thin."

"It's hard to believe, isn't it? It just happened. No dieting, no mind tricks, no struggles with resisting the temptation of food. The pounds just started coming off without any effort on my part. And the weight loss continues, even when I manage to force down the food and all the protein-fortified juice shakes my nutritionist tells me to drink. I'm just skin and bones now."

"That's what happens when you stop eating," said Claire, cautiously.

"But look at how my bones stick out—my rib cage looks like pictures of concentration camp survivors, and I constantly bump against things with my hip bone. My breasts have disappeared, flat as pancakes. And see all the folds of skin hanging from my fanny. How can I ever firm up this skin when I'm not allowed to do any strenuous workouts in the fitness center now?"

"Vivian, the way to make your body look better is to put on some weight."

"I know. Thanks for looking at me. It's a point of reference. Maybe next time you see me you'll see something different and you'll see how far I've come."

"I hope and pray that's true."

Chapter 21

On Easter morning, Claire wanted us to go to church together. We found an Episcopal Church nearby and worshipped there together. Claire explained how the people at her Episcopal Church in Massachusetts were progressive enough to fly a rainbow flag and that meeting with the minister at this church in New Jersey might be helpful. So I decided to make my sister happy by arranging a meeting with him after Claire went back home.

"Tell me, Vivian, what brings you to my office?" asked the middle-aged Rev. Bass when I met with him a week later.

I told him exactly what had happened and how Victor was seeking relationships with gay men.

"Oh? This must be an extremely difficult time for you."

"Actually, this loss has destroyed me on a personal level. I'm functional and never miss a day of work, and I thank God I have a wonderful job. And I'm under the care of a therapist, a nutritionist, and a primary care physician. But I'm having a tough time figuring out how to find some meaning in my life living alone. My faith used to be such an important resource for me, giving me the strength I needed to get through all the other difficult times in my life. Now I feel as if I'm walking through the valley of the shadow of death, as the psalmist would say, without a clue on how to rise above all my despair."

"Have you given up on God?"

"Absolutely not," I said, as I folded my hands, palm to palm, in my lap. "If anything, it feels like God has given up on me. People tell me God doesn't give us more than we can handle. But I have my doubts about that."

"Do you believe in the power of prayer?"

"Yes, I believe we have a personal and loving God who can work through prayer to help us understand His will for our lives. I pray all the time, reminding myself that prayer is as important as breathing."

"Vivian, do you believe in an all-powerful God who is able to transform your husband, delivering him from the bondage of homosexuality and saving your marriage?"

"Wait a minute, you don't understand. The marriage is over. There's no turning back. I still love my husband, but I accept the fact he isn't 100 percent heterosexual. That's not his fault; that's the way he is. It's horrible he never acknowledged his same-gender feelings to me for so many years, but that doesn't mean there's anything wrong with being homosexual. I would never pray to ask God to change Victor's sexual orientation, any more than I would pray to ask God to change his race or age."

"The Bible tells us that 'if you have faith as a grain of mustard seed, you shall say to this mountain, 'Move from here to there,' and it will move; and nothing will be impossible to you,'" said Rev. Bass, quoting the words from Jesus found in the New Testament (Matthew 17:20, RSV). "Are you telling me your faith is so little, not even the size of a grain of mustard seed?"

"I'm not here looking for mountain-moving faith to change Victor's DNA. In fact, I think it takes a lot of God-given courage for Victor to face the truth and come to terms with his sexual orientation. The problem here is me. Look at me, my body is weak and emaciated. Some people tell me I look like I'm dying. I'm struggling to somehow grasp onto something to restore my will to live. And you're talking about praying for God to change my husband's sexual orientation?"

"That seems to me to be the way to save your marriage."

"Well, I'm not seeking salvation for a marriage that's over. It's too late for that. I think that's enough for now. It's time for me to leave."

"Would you like to have a prayer together before you leave?"

"Under the circumstances, I think a moment of silent prayer works for me."

We both bowed our heads for a moment, with me praying fervently for the strength to make a graceful exit without any more drama.

As I drove home, I felt so misunderstood. I had no problem defending Victor's sexual orientation to a stranger and resented the implication from this clergyperson that Victor needed to be fixed. I have a low tolerance for such injustice in the church. Then I pacified myself with the words from Psalm 34:18 (RSV): "The Lord is near to the broken-hearted, and saves the crushed in spirit." *I need to look elsewhere for strength and consolation*, I concluded.

~~~

Later that day I called Claire to fill her in on my visit with Rev. Bass. She was appalled.

"I'm so sorry," said Claire, adding she was flabbergasted by the way Rev. Bass treated me. "He wanted to pray for Victor's deliverance, as if being gay is evil? That's not supposed to happen."

"I keep hearing that phrase—'that's not supposed to happen'—over and over, the story of my life in a nutshell. How ironic. Everyone tells me to focus on Vivian, not Victor. So after I present my situation to this minister, he decides the focus needs to be on God changing Victor. What an idiot! I leave it to someone else to educate that man."

"I had no idea a visit with Rev. Bass would make things worse, not better," said Claire. "But please don't give up. Please take care of yourself."

"I'm trying. I love you, Claire. Gotta hang up now."

~~~

When I mentioned my negative experience with Rev. Bass to Lydia, my next-door neighbor and snow-shoveling companion, she invited me to visit a local Lutheran

Church. I found a warm welcome there. The only drawback was running into Victor's boss and his family, who were active members of this congregation. He greeted me with a look of pathos; no exchange of words necessary.

I decided to forego any more new churchgoing excursions. What I wanted to do was place myself up for adoption. *Wouldn't it be great if a caring person or couple would take me on as a special project on a 24/7 basis, nurturing me back to health and helping me grow through this experience?* I knew it was too far-fetched to think anyone out there with nothing but pure motives would take in a 36-year-old woman with all my baggage.

I needed to look both within myself and beyond myself to find some meaning in my life. That's when I started to develop a craving for poetry. I discovered the poems of Jane Kenyon, Marge Piercy, May Sarton, and Wendy Cope. At last some kindred souls; they may not have any answers for me, but they know how to raise questions about seeking mental clarity in the midst of darkness and turmoil.

I also was bonding with my pet rabbit, Clover—instant delight at first sight. I adored rabbits! As Victor knew so well, I had a long history of finding solace with a rabbit in my arms, including adopting a series of three rabbits—Peter Rabbit (a Dutch breed), Butterscotch (a mixed breed), and Pierre Lapin (a French Lop)—earlier in our marriage. It was a bit tricky at first to manage the logistics of Champ and Clover coexisting in the same space. I trained Champ not to torment Clover in her bunny house, which was secure in the kitchen, but I always had to be on guard so Champ wouldn't resort to her rabbit-chasing instincts when Clover was in my lap or hopping around the floor. Somehow I made it work.

Having a rabbit was a rite of passage in my family, according to my animal-loving father. He made sure each of his four daughters had a pet rabbit. He gave me mine—a large, white New Zealand rabbit with pink eyes—when I was eight years old. She lived in a rabbit hutch that my father built in the backyard. I named her "Bunny Boo," although my mother referred to her as my crying towel and called her "Bunny Boo Hoo." Whenever I felt misunderstood or lonely or sad or otherwise out of sorts, I would scoop up Bunny Boo and hold her for hours. She never told my secrets and just kept twitching her nose, no matter what chaos was going on in my little girl life. I've always felt a sense of well-being holding a rabbit.

In addition to my pets (which I learned in therapy were "love objects"), it occurred to me I needed to strike up friendships with women who enjoyed being single, not misfits wallowing in self-pity nor women who didn't like men, but women who found satisfaction in living alone. *Where, oh where, can I find such role models?* I started by being on the lookout for such women.

~~~

When my writers group needed a place for our monthly gatherings, I volunteered my townhome. I had plenty of room and adequate parking; it was a good opportunity to see if I could play hostess by myself to a small group of people who knew very little about my personal life. Outside of my job assignments, I was writing poems, short stories, and personal essays at that time. Everyone in this eclectic group of men and women seemed wrapped up in their own lives, eager for feedback on whatever piece of writing they were ready to present. And people showed up, read their writing, discussed the work, and drank the coffee I served.

One of the poets named Nathan made the observation that was obvious to all who took a look around my place: "Vivian, you live alone?"

I was glad he cared enough to ask the question so I could make it clear that I was on my own.

"Sadly, I don't have a husband anymore," I said, as I stuffed my hands in the pockets of my denim skirt. "But I have Champ and Clover, as well as a ton of books, which I consider my friends. I hardly call that living alone." *Another baby step forward*, I told myself.

~~~

At work, I received a marvelous assignment: I was invited to travel to Austin, Texas, along with others, to meet with former Texas Congresswoman Barbara Jordan, who had agreed to serve as chair of the Foundation's Advisory Council to champion its national interfaith initiative. Designed to promote caregiver projects in hundreds of communities across the United States, this initiative was focused on helping volunteers provide services to neighbors with chronic health conditions so they could remain in their communities and live independently.

I had two weeks to prepare for my role, which was to attend the meeting and assess how the Foundation's communications objectives could best be achieved through the new leadership of this Advisory Council. My job was to absorb every talking point and nuance, collect sound bites, and identify the strengths and weaknesses of our communications strategy. I was exuberant about having this opportunity to see Barbara Jordan, up close and personal. She was the greatest female orator of our times, in my opinion. I was riding high at the thought of meeting this extraordinary woman with such a legacy of personal strength and spirit. *What a treat!* I rejoiced. *I'm going to Texas to meet Barbara Jordan!*

Chapter 22

After my flight from Newark landed in Austin, Texas, I slung my carry-on garment bag over my shoulder, grabbed my briefcase, and shuffled out of the airplane, navigating my way through the long, cavernous corridors of the airport terminal. As I approached the exit, I saw a display of watercolor paintings encased in glass—an entire wall of exquisite paintings of rabbits greeted me. I considered this a good omen for my visit there. A local artist, Don Kent, really captured the essence of the rabbit—perky eyes, expressive ears, oval-shaped body, soft fur, and a fluffy tail. He painted rabbits romping in the garden, munching on green clover, periscoping above tall grass, and snuggling close together for warmth, comfort, and affection. These depictions of rabbits exuded contentment. *That's what I want in my life*, I told myself. I jotted down the artist's name and contact information and hailed a cab to my hotel.

My arrival the night before the Advisory Council meeting with Barbara Jordan allowed time for me to stroll around Austin, where I made another fortuitous discovery. While browsing the poetry section of a small bookstore, I found a slim volume of poems entitled *Bunny* by a local poet, Susan Bright. I thumbed through some of the pages; the poems were stark, somewhat dark, and dealt with themes that resonated with me, including such titles as "First Love," "Consolation," and "Hungry." *A perfect souvenir*, I thought, as I scooped up an autographed copy and paid for it.

I had done my homework in preparing for this assignment in Texas. I was familiar with Barbara Jordan's dynamic six-year career serving in the United States Congress, as well as her powerful voice speaking out on justice, ethics, and integrity. I had vivid memories of her spellbinding keynote address at the 1976 Democratic Convention when I was a 20-year-old college student watching her on television in a crowded campus lounge. She knew how to make all sorts of breakthroughs in life.

As I researched books, articles, and speeches about her, I learned Barbara Jordan had suffered since 1973 from "progressively debilitating neurological impairments, about which she will not comment." It was later divulged that her range of physical ailments was staggering: multiple sclerosis, leukemia, diabetes, hypertension, and pneumonia.

Barbara Jordan helped others dismiss the presence of her wheelchair, commenting that people are "interested in my words, not my feet." A large black woman with great intellect and an engaging smile, she understood the power of words.

When members of the 13-person Advisory Council and Foundation representatives gathered the next morning around a large, wooden conference table in a function room of the hotel, Barbara Jordan made her entrance with broadcast-quality flair. "We have before us an extraordinary opportunity," she began, with her impeccable enunciation, "and now is the time to take action in this ministry of caring." She spoke with a strong sense of purpose, concluding her opening remarks with these words: "We can't afford to fail. I do not tolerate failure."

The strength of her convictions and quality of her mind, as well as her voice combined with her in-your-face charisma, inspired action. When she rubbed her hands together and said, "I'm sitting here all lathered up about this idea," I could feel her energy. I discovered when you spend time in the presence of someone with such clarity of purpose, your own longing for clarity grows stronger.

In my research I had learned she had grown up with a strong sense of self, following her grandfather's advice: "You just trot your own horse and don't get into the same rut as everyone else." She dared to be different—to follow her dreams and beliefs. She had a high regard for the magnificent power of the mind, exhorting others to "think clearly, argue persuasively—in that order" and "do not call for black power or green power; call for brain power."

I left that gathering uplifted. Barbara Jordan had touched my life as I witnessed firsthand her unwavering spirit and her resolve to take action. My brief encounter with her was a personal wake-up call to get back on track; it was time to embrace the possibilities in my life and move forward.

On the airplane trip back to New Jersey, I opened up my new poetry book and discovered this poem by Susan Bright:

Repairs

Bunny
was closed for repairs,
damaged
someplace
deeper than
her heart,
someplace
dark and diffuse,
that
fire and galaxies flew
out of.

She
slammed doors
and hung up a sign
that said,
Closed for Repairs.

She
stayed closed for 12 years:
144 months,
105,120 hours,
6,307,200 minutes
378,432,000 healing breaths—
after which
she turned
the sign
back over.

It said,
Open for Repairs.

Hey, this poem is for me, I told myself. *That's precisely what I need to do. I need to be "open for repairs," not "closed for repairs."*

Part of me wanted to believe the events and circumstances of this visit to Texas were signs that God was reaching out to me in far more creative ways than I could imagine. *I can't allow a failed marriage to defeat or define who I am,* I coached myself. I needed to find the strength and courage to define my own worth. I needed to rise above all the morbid inclinations, shame, and despair. I needed to find some meaning in this experience and move on with my life.

~~~

When I returned home, I felt the stirrings of a renewed sense of hopefulness. I contacted Don Kent in Texas and, delighted to find his artwork was affordable, ordered his watercolor entitled "Bunny Bunch." I also flipped through some mail order catalogues I had added to a pile in the Things-To-Do room. I came across a full ensemble of comforter, duster, shams, sheets, and matching curtains in a flowered pattern of violets with green scalloped leaves against a white background that had a purple-ribboned border and white eyelet lace. I could picture myself luxuriating in this crisp and vibrant bedding. It wasn't the most dog-friendly color scheme, but Champ's perpetual shedding of black fur was the least of my concerns. I placed my order and anticipated its arrival within the next week. *I can sleep in flowered sheets now,* I told myself, as I recalled some obscure prohibition I had followed about wives not making husbands sleep in bedding decorated with flowers—as if sleeping in flowered sheets had a feminizing effect on a man. *Where did that nonsense come from?*

~~~

I was eager to share something positive for a change when I met with Dr. Barley two days later on a Friday afternoon. He welcomed my insights, but then took our conversation in another direction.

"Vivian, I want you to see an expert on eating disorders in Philadelphia. You continue to lose weight, even though your food logs show you're eating three meals a day and not doing any strenuous workouts. Maybe I'm missing something that needs to be done to reverse your weight loss. Are you willing to meet with this expert?"

"Of course, I'll do whatever you say."

"Dr. Stilts runs a highly respected inpatient program for people with eating disorders. I want him to do an assessment of you and review our plan of care, which doesn't appear to be working for you right now."

"You think I might have to be hospitalized? But I've just had this amazing experience in Texas to jumpstart my recovery."

"I want to prepare you for the possibility that you may need to spend some time in the hospital. I'm glad you feel a lift in your spirits. But your body is lagging way behind."

"What about my job? What about Champ and Clover? No, that's not what I want. Trust me. I'll try harder. I'll try twice as hard, or three or 10 times as hard, to eat what I'm told to eat by my nutritionist. I'm drinking the protein-fortified juice shakes and taking the vitamin supplements, as well as my medications."

"I know you're trying, but I think things have gone too far. That's why we need an assessment from Dr. Stilts."

"Okay, I'll go see this expert. I don't want you to get into trouble. But I have no interest in a hospital stay if I can possibly avoid it. I'll schedule an appointment to see Dr. Stilts as soon as possible."

~~~

Later that night was my turn to host my writers group. Six people showed up. I served coffee and dessert on my cherished cobalt blue-and-white Dedham Rabbit reproduction plates. Victor had given me various pieces of this pottery pattern over the years as birthday, anniversary, and Christmas gifts. We wanted the full complement of The Potting Shed product line, crafted in Concord, Massachusetts, by our 25th wedding anniversary. *Another dream turns to dust in the wind*, I pondered while I took these items from the china cabinet Victor would take possession of when the distribution of property agreement was finalized. I felt my life had become a series of disappointments.

After the meeting, Nathan—a good-natured man who wrote superb poetry, was a high school English teacher, had attended the last four gatherings, and always had something interesting to say about everyone's writing—lingered behind.

"Would you like me to stay and help you with the dishes, Vivian?" he said, allowing others to hear his intentions.

"A poet volunteering to help clean up? That doesn't happen every day. Sure, I'll take all the help I can get," I replied.

"Do you want me to stick around, too?" asked Fred, the group leader, in a paternalistic manner.

"Nathan, what do you think? Should Fred stick around as my body guard?" I said, rather flippantly.

"No, I'm harmless tonight," Nathan joked. "I've already met my quota this month for doing creepy things to rabbit-loving women with little black dogs."

157

"Looks like you're off the hook, Fred," I said. "Thanks for looking out for me. I'll be fine."

When everyone else had left, Nathan started to stack up the dishes in the dining room and made several trips back and forth to the kitchen—handling the dishes with great care—while I started filling the sink with water and squeezed a generous dab of dishwashing liquid under the faucet.

"Hey, it's sweet of you to help with the dishes," I said, eager for kindness and positive attention from a man. "I certainly can handle this by myself, but I appreciate the gesture."

"Well, it's kind of you to open up your home for the group. You have a nice place here."

"It's a polite and respectful group of people. We all seem to get along."

"The more I see you, the more I think you could use a good friend these days," said Nathan, grabbing a dish towel to dry the dishes.

"Well, you're right about that. A good friend with a ton of patience and understanding who is willing to take me on as a project—yes. But a boyfriend? No way. I'm certainly not girlfriend material at this point."

"What do you mean?"

"As you can see, I'm a walking skeleton right now. Actually, I'm in danger of being put in the hospital if I can't manage to put some weight back on real soon."

"That sounds serious," said Nathan, in his deep low-pitched voice.

"Remember the story of Hansel and Gretel, when the wicked witch in the forest keeps trying to fatten them up after she takes them prisoner? Those kids were so clever to present sticks instead of their arms for her inspection. Well, I need a wicked witch with gingerbread and cakes to fatten me up."

"I've been in some tough spots myself," he said. "I won't bore you with the details, but I know a few things about being lonely in the forest."

"That comes through in some of your poems."

"A good friend can be helpful."

"Well, thanks for the advice."

"Listen, I've been going to some poetry readings at a bookstore in Middlesex County called The Bookworm's Delight. They have a great poet coming from Brooklyn next Thursday evening. Would you like to come along?"

"I'm not sure if I'm available. It depends on how things go in Philadelphia next Tuesday."

"How about I call you on Wednesday?"

"Okay."

"Great. I'll give you a call then. Maybe I can be the wicked witch and feed you some cake. They serve delicious desserts there, along with strong coffee."

"We'll see about that. Strong coffee are the magic words for me," I said, as Champ came up from behind with her carrot squeaky toy in her mouth.

"That's my cue to make my exit now. I don't want to overstay my welcome."

"Thanks for your helping hand."

"It's my pleasure. Good night, Vivian."

"Goodnight, Nathan."

I walked him to the door, turned the deadbolt lock, watched him walk down the driveway, and then shut off the outdoor lights after he drove away in his solid-black Chevrolet Blazer—a heavy-duty vehicle designed to conquer rugged terrain.

Chapter 23

The following Tuesday afternoon I took a train to Philadelphia and then a cab to Dr. Stilts's address. I felt nervous and apprehensive about the visit; I dreaded placing myself in this unfamiliar territory.

Fueled by caffeine and adrenaline, I climbed up the stairs despite my weakened physical condition and checked in with the receptionist. Then I sat on a folding chair in the waiting room and pulled out from my briefcase a book I had purchased from my mail order book club entitled *Take This Book to the Hospital With You: A Consumer Guide to Surviving Your Hospital Stay* by Charles Inlander and Ed Weiner. Although I was determined to avoid a hospital stay, I wanted to be prepared in case things didn't go my way. This book claimed to serve as a passport for hospital patients—especially first-timers such as me—who find themselves "strangers in a strange land." Comparisons were made to feeling like "a vacationing traveler who blithely and unknowingly wanders across a border into a combat zone"; this was a guide on how to "tiptoe safely through the medical minefield and make it back home intact."

I had just read the paragraph about "nothing could be more hazardous to your health than being a passively compliant patient" when Dr. Stilts greeted me and invited me into his office. A tall, gangly man dressed in a white laboratory coat with deep pockets, this psychiatrist gave me a warm smile and proceeded to ask me dozens of questions about my medical history, various behavioral and lifestyle issues, and current circumstances relating to my recent weight loss, clinical depression, treatment plan, and medication use. I answered all of his questions—honestly.

"Would you step up to the scales so I can check your weight today?" he asked.

"Of course I will," I replied. "Am I allowed to see you weigh me or do I need to keep my eyes closed?"

"You can see for yourself what the scales show," he said.

I assumed he was already aware that I had been restricted from weighing myself and knowing about the fluctuations in numbers measuring my weight loss. My primary care physician had imposed this restriction to help me avoid engaging in the self-sabotage mind games characteristic of some individuals with eating disorders.

Then we sat near his desk to review his assessment.

"Vivian, you weigh 106 pounds today," said Dr. Stilts. "That's 78 percent of your ideal weight, based on your height. And that's not good enough."

He went on to explain anorexia nervosa is a life-threatening eating disorder that is diagnosed when a person weighs at least 15 percent less than his or her normal body weight, resulting from self-starvation and excessive weight loss. He declared me eligible for his inpatient program, which offers a structured environment where all meals were under strict supervision along with individual, group, and family therapy three times a week.

"Based on what you've told me, I question if you can really make enough changes on your own to do what's necessary to restore your health," he added.

"Oh, but I can," I responded. "I am the queen of structure."

"You must be far more aggressive about your food intake. Now you're taking in about 1,000 to 2,000 calories a day. But you should work up to taking in 3,000-plus calories a day."

"I don't really count calories. I just try to eat whatever I can and write it down in my food log."

"Regarding your medication, it seems you've experienced almost all of the bad side effects of Elavil without any of the benefits of its antidepressant purpose. I recommend a switch to another antidepressant called Paxil."

"Okay, I can do that."

"Vivian, I can admit you to our program here. We can help you."

"No, that's not what I want. I'm not doing anything without first talking to Dr. Barley. Furthermore, you need to know a few things about me we didn't cover yet."

"Really? I have enough information to make a diagnosis."

"But I'm not some kind of Karen Carpenter or supermodel wannabe who tries to look like Twiggy. I'm not obsessed with my body size. I don't think I would fit in with a bunch of teenagers who are fixated on their appearance."

"The mean age of individuals in our program is 24 to 25 years old."

"Yes, and I'm 36 years old. I have responsibilities, and I'm on my own. So family therapy doesn't apply to me. Okay, so I've had a major setback in my personal life. Perhaps not eating is a way to gain some sense of control when everything else in my life is stressful and overwhelming. But this is all just temporary."

"But I understand your rapid weight loss has been going on for the past four months," said Dr. Stilts, as he checked his clipboard.

"That's true. But I consider my condition to be 'situational anorexia.' Not eating has more to do with my will to live, not some code that appears in the *Diagnostic and Statistical Manual of Mental Disorders*. I believe my desire for food can be a metric for my will to live. No desire for food plus despair equals no will to live. So the best treatment plan for me is to build up my will to live. I think I can make that happen on an outpatient basis. I have a whole team of healthcare professionals who really care about me. And I've already started to turn a corner in my thinking during this past week."

"I'm glad to hear you're motivated to make some changes. But it needs to happen now. You are in serious trouble."

"Thank you for your time and your advice," I jumped in to help him wrap up this visit. "I'm sure you'll be talking to Dr. Barley, too. I'm determined to bounce back as soon as I can."

"Okay, I wish you well," said Dr. Stilts as he escorted me to the receptionist so I could write out a check to pay for my visit. He also arranged for a cab to pick me up and take me to the train station so I could return back home. *That was a close call,* I sighed with relief. *Too close for comfort.*

~~~

From that point on, I forced myself to eat whatever I could. And when Nathan called on Wednesday, I agreed to go with him to the poetry reading on Thursday. He arrived at 6:00 p.m., popped inside to greet Champ and Clover, and then whisked me away to the bookstore, where he ordered a thick slice of Linzer Torte to go along with my large mug of black coffee.

"You'll share this with me, right?" I asked, as I grabbed two forks and a knife to cut the pastry in half. "I seem to eat better when I'm eating with someone."

"So now who's force-feeding whom?" said Nathan.

"I'm allowed. It gives me a sense of control, which is a good thing for me these days."

Together, we devoured the entire piece of Linzer Torte.

The poetry reading was inspirational and sparked lots of lively conversation between Nathan and me. I realized that I enjoyed being with him. He was easygoing and made no demands. He liked my pets.

"Are you doing anything special this weekend?" he asked as he drove me back to my house.

"No special plans for Memorial Day weekend except focusing on somehow working up to 3,000 calories a day. How about you?"

"I'm available to watch you do some eating, if you like."

"In that case, how about coming over to my place Saturday or Sunday? We can pick up a movie at the video store and maybe even order a pizza. A pizza! I haven't had pizza in months. That's not something I would do alone. But it would look great on my food log."

"Yes, that's a great idea. What time do you want me to come by?"

"Bring a book to read and come at 4:00 p.m. But remember, it's not a date. I'm not dating. We're just friends."

"Okay, I'll see you Saturday."

~~~

On Friday I went to my primary care physician's office for a weigh-in at noontime before my session with Dr. Barley.

"So are we playing hardball today?" I asked as I walked into Dr. Barley's office, anticipating a heavy-duty session.

"We have serious business to discuss," said Dr. Barley, in a somber manner.

He reviewed my situation, including the content of his consultation with Dr. Stilts.

"Vivian, I need you to look at me. Eye contact. Stay with me. This is important."

I assumed my eyeball-to-eyeball gaze, on heightened alert.

"Vivian, your body is very weak. Your weight loss has gone too far. I see you slipping away right before my eyes. You are on the path to self-destruction. And I really don't want to lose you..." Then his voice trailed off.

"I know things have gone too far," I said in a quivering voice. I was moved by the compassion and empathy I saw in his face. He really cared about me and was doing his best to communicate the gravity of my physical condition.

"It takes more than the work we do in this office to bring you back," he confessed. "You have a serious condition that can take you out. If saving your life means spending some time in the hospital, then that's what you need to do."

I was taken aback by his sincerity and outpouring of genuine emotion. Whether it was a matter of transference or mystical thinking or dissociative reverie, I could easily picture my father at that moment, lovingly reaching out to me with the truth and gently persuading me to first hang on as I dangled over the cliff and then inch my way back to safety. As a young girl, I had witnessed how the relentless spread of cancer had taken him down, causing his body to wither away to an anorexic state like mine at the end when all treatments had failed. These visualizations prompted a flood of tears as I imagined how heartbroken Daddy would be to see his grown-up little girl in such dire circumstances.

Dr. Barley stepped over to sit in the chair next to mine and placed his hand on my shoulder as I sobbed. I finally looked up and noticed he had tears in his eyes, too. That made me cry even harder.

"Let it go, let all the tears flow," he told me.

So I did.

I felt a tremendous release as I cried, no longer trying to minimize my profound sadness and despair. It was an emotional cleansing for me.

"Okay, so now we know I can cry about all this," I said at last, as I regained some measure of composure. "You know, my father would tell me, 'Be strong.'"

"Yes he would, Vivian."

"Listen, I honestly feel I've had some sort of breakthrough, now and since my trip to Texas. I really believe I can make a comeback. How about this? Before you drag me kicking and screaming to Dr. Stilts's program in Philadelphia, how about giving me one last chance to prove what I can do?"

So we talked some more. I could tell from the twists and turns of our conversation that this was a difficult judgment call for Dr. Barley to make, whether to proceed with the plans he had lined up for my hospitalization or to allow a little more time for me to change.

I was terrified by my impending hospitalization and agreed to all of Dr. Barley's terms. For starters, I made a commitment to eat three balanced meals every day, without fail, no matter what—with weekly weigh-ins at my primary care physician's office to track my progress. I also agreed to call in every day and leave a message on Dr. Barley's answering machine, reporting I had consumed my three meals that day. Furthermore, I made a commitment to do whatever it took to take better care of myself. Self-deprivation was totally unacceptable from that moment forward.

"I'm a fighter," I declared. "I follow through on my commitments. I don't go around disappointing people. I can do this. Now."

"That's the deal," said Dr. Barley.

"Watch me. I can walk the talk. I promise to make this happen."

I was so grateful Dr. Barley, my lifeline, hadn't given up on me yet.

Chapter 24

The uphill battle to feed myself, mouthful by mouthful, was hard work.

I watched Champ in awe. She wolfed down every opened can of Mighty Dog I dumped in her dog bowl within 30 seconds. Then she spent several minutes lapping up any traces of food that stuck to her bowl, sliding it around the kitchen floor in her zeal for another smidgen of sustenance. I also studied how Clover devoured her carrot sticks, starting at one end and keeping a steady pace as she nibbled and swallowed her way to the very end. Basic creature instincts.

Yet eating had become a dreaded chore for me. I preferred the addictive state of emptiness and the numbing effect of gnawing hunger, which gave me a twisted sense of control as the master, not the slave, of my existence.

I tackled the task at hand: eating a bowl of oatmeal. I had the physical dexterity to prepare my food and set everything up in front of me—the bowl, the oatmeal, the spoon. I could lift the spoonful of cooked oatmeal to my lips, take it in, and move it around inside my mouth. I tried to imagine how good it felt on frigid Vermont mornings when my Swedish grandmother made oatmeal, pouring cream on top and serving it with a bowl of fresh homemade applesauce on the side. Everyone could taste the love in her comfort food, which I believed as a little girl made our stomachs smile and kept us feeling warm inside the entire morning. I savored the fond memory and coached myself to swallow—that was the hardest part. I paused to congratulate myself and then carved out the next spoonful to eat. Then I repeated the same tedious sequence of actions over and over. Sometimes it took 30 minutes to force it all down.

My new mantra was "food is fuel." I pictured my car running on empty—the nail-biting anxiety it caused and the sheer relief of finding a gas station in the nick of time—and then hearing the gurgle of gas being pumped into the gas tank.

Food is fuel—I don't have to taste it or enjoy it; I just have to swallow it, I told myself. Then I could write it down in my food log and move onto something else more interesting until the next meal. I also decided I needed to start treating my protein-fortified juice shakes as a supplement, not a meal replacement. I drank this mixture and then ate a toasted English muffin slathered with peanut butter four hours later.

~~~

Nathan came over late Saturday afternoon and spent several hours with me. We talked and read books together and drank coffee. Then we called to order a pizza with extra cheese and stopped at the video store. We strolled the aisles, comparing notes on which movies we had seen and our personal preferences. Nathan liked "shoot 'em up" movies and mysteries whereas I liked drama and psychological thrillers. We narrowed the choices down to a Clint Eastwood movie or a Woody Allen movie. Then I spotted *Drop Dead Fred* on the shelf.

"Let's get this one," I said. "It's about a woman whose life falls apart and the return of her imaginary friend from childhood. It may look like a children's movie, but I read it has some adult themes. And no blood and gore."

When we returned to my place, we cut up some fresh vegetables together and sautéed them in the skillet for our pizza topping. Nathan transferred pieces from the pizza box to our plates: one slice for me and one slice for him. Our plan was to eat in the family room and arrange our food on the coffee table so we could start watching the movie.

"What would you like to drink with your pizza—a beer, some wine, or a Coke?" I asked.

"A Coke, thank you very much," he said.

I grabbed a cold can of Coke from the refrigerator and handed it to him, along with a tall glass with ice cubes. Then I pulled out a can of Diet Pepsi for myself.

Nathan frowned at my choice of beverage but said nothing.

I started to eat my slice of pizza with a fork and knife, cutting it up in bite-sized pieces, whereas Nathan lifted his slice up to his mouth with his hand and ate heartily. Within minutes, he was ready for a second slice.

"Shall I bring you another Coke?" I asked.

"I prefer the Diet Pepsi this round."

"Really? But you don't have a weight problem."

"It's a habit," he said. "I'm more used to drinking diet drinks."

"You know, so am I. My sister-in-law had a fit when she came to visit me and found a case of Diet Pepsi in my refrigerator. But regular soda tastes too sweet for me."

"I see—," said Nathan, hesitantly.

"Oh, I see what you mean. Maybe I should switch to juice and forget about the no-calorie drinks for now."

"Brilliant deduction, my dear Watson," said Nathan, with a gesture pretending to smoke a pipe like Sherlock Holmes.

We watched the movie as I finished my pizza.

"I did it," I said. "And it was good. Thanks for being my food watcher and eating companion tonight."

"I'm glad I can help. You did all the work. Good pizza, great company, and a rather entertaining movie."

"Well, don't get too attached to this monster TV," I said. "It belongs to Victor, who will take it away one of these days."

"So let's enjoy it as long as we can. Hey, do you have any interest in boxing?"

"Not really."

"I love to watch boxing on Tuesday nights," he said.

"Well, come on over on Tuesday night, if you like. Maybe I'll pick up a few tips from watching boxing, now that

I'm in fighter mode. Besides, you can be on food watcher duty again. Your presence helps me make the food disappear."

"That's a great idea. I'll come over for some rock 'em, sock 'em boxing. Perhaps we can make it a Tuesday night habit?"

"Perhaps. So you teach high school students all day long about the classics in literature, such as Shakespeare, Kafka, and Poe; you read Kierkegaard and Wittgenstein for fun; and you write jaw-dropping poetry. But you like shoot 'em up movies and boxing. You are a man of many mysteries, Nathan."

"Not so many mysteries, really," he said, with a tinge of sadness in his voice.

"Well, I turn into a pumpkin at 10:00 p.m. these days," I said. "So it's time for me to say 'Good Night.'"

"Okay. See you Tuesday night. Boxing starts at 8 o'clock."

"Come earlier, if you like, and bring your book. Thanks again."

Champ and I escorted Nathan to the front door as he made his exit. It was fun to pal around with someone and focus on the here and now, not the painful past or the uncertain future.

~~~

I reported my progress to Dr. Barley on a daily basis, went for my weekly weigh-in, and met with Dr. Barley for my two weekly sessions. Nathan did come over on Tuesday evening for boxing. And I had a full week of interesting work at the Foundation. I was off to a good start, doing what I needed to do to stay out of the hospital.

~~~

When Nathan suggested we ride together to our writers group on Friday night, I accepted. On the way home, he asked if I would like to go out for drinks.

"Sure. There's a place on Route 202 that doesn't look too shabby," I said, eager to spend as much time as I could with Nathan to enjoy his company.

We were seated at a table for two. I ordered a gin and tonic; Nathan ordered a club soda.

All of a sudden it started to feel as if we were having a date; it was romantic to be out in public as a couple. But I dismissed this notion, reminding myself we were only friends.

"Was this a test to make sure I ordered something with more calories than a Diet Pepsi, or are you showing me that you're the stoic one by being the designated driver tonight?" I asked, making eye-to-eye contact.

"Neither. It's only 9:30 p.m., and I thought you might like to go out for a drink."

"This is new territory for me," I said, feeling at ease with him to reveal more about myself. "I haven't had any alcohol for months. I've always thought a bar is a good place to meet someone with a drinking problem, which is the last thing I need in my life. So I don't go out to bars to meet people."

"Oh?"

"You look like you know your way around a liquor cabinet, Nathan. Why the club soda tonight?"

"Actually, alcohol and I are no longer friends."

I was confused.

"So why are we here having drinks?"

"It's okay for you to have a drink, if you like," he said.

"Are you telling me you never drink alcohol now?"

"That's right," he said. "I've been sober for three years now."

"Why, that's fabulous!" I felt as if I had hit the jackpot. "It's so refreshing to spend time with someone with a clear mind, unclouded by alcohol."

"Well, I've never received that sort of reaction," he said with a chuckle. "You see my sobriety as a positive?"

"You better believe it! I adore being with a man who doesn't drink. Forget the gin and tonic, which I ordered just to be polite. Let's ditch this place and find a diner for coffee."

"Okay. Sounds good to me."

He dropped a crisp ten dollar bill on the table before we made our getaway.

~~~

We decided to hang out together on Saturday night at my place. I was looking forward to another good time with Nathan. He arrived early in the evening.

"I have a treat for us tonight," I said.

"Oh yeah?"

"I stopped at my favorite bakery and picked up an apple strudel with some sort of cheesecake filling to go with our coffee. I'm sure it has a zillion calories, just what I need."

"Let's give it a try," he said.

I dished out our strudel. We both tasted it. It was absolutely delicious.

"This is outrageously good," said Nathan, licking his fork. "Is this your way of seducing me?"

"Seducing you? I don't have a clue how to do that. But I admit this is rather orgasmic, huh?"

"That's an interesting adjective for you to use."

"Believe it or not, I can be an affectionate and fun-loving person. Even playful. You haven't really seen that side of me yet, huh?"

"Are you flirting with me?" he asked.

"We're just having a conversation. In fact, it's probably a good time to talk about what's going on between us. I really like you, Nathan. I consider you a gift. You think there's a chance our friendship can grow into something else?"

I looked into his eyes, hoping to see a glimmer of interest.

"What do you think, Vivian?"

"I have a hunch you like being around me. I also think you're waiting for me to make the first move, should we decide to become romantically involved."

He paused and stared at me as if he was gazing at the stars.

"I know you've been hurt very badly by Victor. It's going to take some time for you to ever trust another man. But when that happens, I'll be there for you."

I felt my heart flutter like a butterfly. But then I felt the sting of uncertainty.

"First of all, you need to be totally honest with me. How can I ever be sure whether or not any man is gay? I wish there was some sort of litmus test for figuring out if a man has even one gay bone in his body."

"Well, I can assure you that when it comes to physical attraction, I like women, not men," he said.

I believed him. Nothing about him made me think he had any questions about his heterosexual preferences.

"And what about me?" I said. "You think there's a chance there could be any chemistry between us?"

"Oh Lord, yes," he said with a grin. "I've grown very fond of you. I find you intoxicating, if I may be so bold to use that word. I almost have the courage to tell you how I feel. But I don't want to scare you away."

"I feel safe with you, Nathan. I'm so grateful to have you in my life now. As you can see, I have a long way to go before my body returns to some sort of voluptuous feminine shape. In so many ways, you probably see me as some sort of overgrown teenager. But I assure you my body mechanics are just fine, thank you very much. All of my female body parts are in working order. And there's nothing fragile about my ability to give and receive affection."

"That's wonderful news to me," he said.

"So when the spirit moves, why don't we try a kiss?"

I leaned toward him. He leaned toward me. We kissed, gently at first and then with more passion. It felt so wonderful to be in the arms of a man again. It felt good. It felt healing. It felt right, as if some sort of reawakening could happen. *Why don't I just go with my feelings for a change?* I told myself. *No analysis, no weighing of the pros and cons, no wrestling with morality angst. Just be spontaneous.*

"Listen, I've got an idea," I said, feeling wild and adventurous. "How about taking a hot bubble bath together?"

"Now?"

"Yes, now. Let's hop in the bathtub and see what happens."

"Are you sure?"

"Yes I'm sure," I said. "Let's do it."

So we did.

Chapter 25

The following week I traveled to Asheville, North Carolina, for a two-day national meeting on improving the recruitment and distribution of primary care providers, especially for underserved populations.

I thought I was doing well. But then I woke up in my hotel room when Hannah, a colleague from the Foundation's financial office, called me on the telephone to see why I was late meeting her in the dining room for breakfast before the national meeting started. I had overslept and was alarmed by my failure to be up and dressed for the day.

I quickly pulled myself together. I greeted Hannah and walked over to the breakfast buffet to select a huge bran muffin. I placed the muffin on a plate and then transferred it to a tray. As I slid the tray down the metal shelf of the cafeteria-style serving line, I came to the end of the line and tried to pick up the tray. But I was unable to lift the tray off the shelf because my wrists went limp; I didn't have enough muscle control to handle the weight of the tray. I tried again, only this time the tray and plate crashed to the floor. A kitchen worker came over and picked up the mess, while I stared dumbfounded by my lack of strength.

"I'm so sorry," I said.

"No problem. I'll take care of this," said the kitchen worker.

I went over to Hannah's table.

"Did you see what just happened? The muscles in my wrists and arms aren't working today. This has never happened before. Maybe I'm still asleep or having some sort of medication reaction or something?"

"Sit down. I'll bring you some breakfast," said Hannah.

This episode passed, but I could see Hannah was concerned about me. So was I. From that point on I made sure to eat and be careful about how I moved around. I tried to reassure Hannah throughout the business trip that I was okay. But I didn't think I was convincing. I later found out she had shared her concerns about my health with others at the office. I don't blame her; it was scary for both of us.

~~~

When I arrived home on Friday night, I received a telephone call from Nathan.

"Hey, world traveler, how was your trip?"

I was glad to hear his voice.

"The trip was fine, with a minor incident that has caused some ruckus at work," I said, then filled him in on all the details.

"Are you eating?"

"Yes, I'm eating and doing everything I'm supposed to do. I guess there must be some kind of time lag in coming back from this anorexic state. I may be more fragile than I think."

"I'm thinking it's a good idea for me to keep an eye on you this weekend," he said. "And I'm thinking about taking an overnight trip to upstate New York tomorrow, to check on some property I own there and open up the small trailer I keep in a nearby campground. Would you like to come along and keep me company?"

I was thrilled to accept his invitation. A road trip adventure with Nathan seemed like an excellent getaway.

~~~

Not only was the overnight trip with Nathan a fun experience, but I was ready to declare my will to live had returned. I started to gain some weight, along with my physical strength. My work at the Foundation was going very well, and Nathan made me feel loved and cared for. At last, I was starting to create a life of my own—on my terms.

Then I received a telephone call at 10:30 p.m. on a Tuesday night while Nathan and I were watching boxing on television. It was Victor. His car had broken down, and he was stranded.

"Is there any way you can come and give me a ride home?" he said.

"I have company right now. What about Howard? Can't he give you a ride?"

"It's a long story. But Howard's in the hospital now. I was on my way back home from visiting him when my car broke down. I managed to have it towed to the Honda dealer, but now I have no way to get home. It's late, and it's dark, and nothing's open now. I'm really in a bind."

I was somewhat annoyed but agreed to pick him up. Victor still hadn't found a lawyer to handle our divorce. Nathan offered to come with me, but I decided he didn't need to be part of this drama. Nathan said he would wait for my return, to make sure I was okay.

~~~

I hadn't seen Victor in a couple of months, although he would call me every week or so to keep in touch with me. When I pulled into the parking lot of the Honda dealer, I saw no sign of life except Victor standing in the dark next to a pay phone. I drove up to him, unlocked the passenger door, and restrained Champ while Victor jumped in, clutching the contents of a big paper bag under his arm.

Champ jumped all over Victor, showering him with doggy kisses. Victor greeted Champ and somehow juggled her and the bag in his lap.

"Champ's so glad to see you. She really misses you."

"I miss her, too. And Vivian, I can't thank you enough for doing this for me."

"I hope you would do the same for me. And you're lucky I just happen to be at home, not away on a business trip."

"I'm glad you came, but I don't feel so lucky these days."

"So what's in the bag?"

177

"Oh, I brought some six-packs of beer for Howard in the hospital. I know that's what I would want if I was the one in the hospital."

"They let you bring beer into the hospital?"

"Not really. That's why I'm bringing it back home with me."

"Is Howard dying?"

"No, nothing like that. He'll be discharged soon."

"I'd just as soon you spare me the details."

"Actually, his wife works at the hospital."

"Howard has a wife?"

"Yes, and an adopted son who is a teenager now."

"Boy, your life has become complicated. Are you happy?"

"Yes, I'm happy with Howard—"

"Okay, that's enough. I don't want to hear any more about you and Howard."

We chatted some more as I drove him to his apartment. Victor told me his parents were coming to New Jersey in July and that they weren't so sure they wanted to meet Howard yet. I hoped I would see Victor's parents during their visit.

"Again, thanks for the ride," he said, after I dropped him off on the sidewalk in front of his place.

"You're welcome. This is one way for Champ to see you haven't disappeared off the face of the earth."

"Not yet. But life in the fast lane has a few bumps. I'll contact a lawyer soon." He told me he found out Zachary's father accepted payment through his employer's legal benefits so he plans to ask him to review the financial agreement my lawyer had sent to him.

"Yes, Victor. The sooner, the better. Everyone tells me that the sooner we take care of this, the less likely things will become nastier."

When I arrived at Victor's apartment, he thanked me again and patted Champ on her head as she took her last licks of him before he climbed out of the car.

I drove home, feeling relieved I had handled this interaction so well. I kept looking for outward signs of Victor's metamorphosis as a gay man, but he pretty much looked and acted the same, even when wearing unfamiliar clothes. The marital glow I usually felt when I was with him was fading; I started looking at him with new eyes and absolutely no desire to be physically touched by him. In fact, I started to feel sorry for him, thinking how hard it must be for him to make adjustments in his new life. The Victor I loved was turning into someone else, a different person with different interests and priorities. It was still hard to let go of the past, and I still felt tremendous unconditional love toward the Victor I knew, but it was becoming easier to let go of the present-day Victor. I could see "the tie that binds us" was unraveling; I could manage to go on and live my life without him as my husband and best friend.

How ironic, I thought. *I came to the rescue for Victor tonight, but I was the one who needed rescuing just a few weeks earlier when my own hospitalization seemed inevitable.* I was grateful Nathan had helped me through my own crisis. It was time to thank Nathan for waiting around for me, send him on his way back home, and call it a night.

Chapter 26

Six months after Victor moved out, I was starting to take control of my life by focusing on taking care of myself. The rhythm of my workflow at the Foundation was challenging, yet more relaxed as many of my colleagues were taking their summer vacations. My Vice President, Jack Briggs, had resigned and moved out of state; I was hopeful Katarina would be promoted to the vacant position because she deserved it and would do outstanding work in that role. My work with Dr. Barley was helping me. I was gaining some weight and body strength at a slow but steady rate, as I inched my way toward shedding my anorexic label.

I stayed in touch with a few friends and neighbors and continued to maintain some of my independent interests, belonging to the local Toastmasters Club and my writers group. Nathan was a marvelous friend, but I was smart enough not to latch on to him too tightly; I had learned my lesson about not becoming too dependent on any man in my life. As a teacher, Nathan was on his summer schedule without any classroom commitments, so he had more time to spend with me. He took a trip to the Bahamas, which he had scheduled months earlier, for part of his summer. Otherwise, he came over to my place two or three evenings a week, depending on my work and travel schedule.

How does a woman living alone take a vacation? I pondered. *Why bother?* I was at a loss to figure out how I would spend my vacation time without a husband. But my sister Noelle, a woman living alone at that time with a long career working for the State of New Hampshire, came up with an answer and invited me to spend a week with her at the beach in Maine.

Up until this time, the idea of two sisters taking a vacation together didn't occur to either of us. As sisters with an age difference of 14 years, we rarely spent much time together on our own. Noelle, the oldest of five children, left home after high school for a job in the city—100 miles away—when I, her baby sister, started kindergarten. Over the years we had been long-distance sisters, with anywhere from 300 to 3,000 miles between our doorsteps. We did whatever it took to join various family gatherings during the holidays, masterminding the juggling of hectic schedules and coaxing our husbands to go along with the whirlwind travel plans required to make it happen. We would have telephone conversations during periods of personal crisis, coaching one another to be strong through the painful times and reminding ourselves of our Swedish heritage with the admonition, "We are Vikings!" And we would somehow cope with the family undercurrents of change and conflict. Without exception, such interactions would center on helping the family member in greatest need at the moment—usually not the two of us. Little energy remained for the pure enjoyment of being sisters.

Noelle made arrangements for us to stay in Kennebunkport, not far from President Bush's compound. We established some ground rules for the week: (1) Thou shalt not discuss family problems or analyze unresolved issues from the past; (2) Thou shalt strive for simplicity, shunning all contact with our employers; and (3) Thou shalt fill thy days with pleasurable activities, including early morning walks and cycling, lounging on the beach, finding treasures in the shops, pondering the beauty and wisdom of life, reading books, drinking coffee, taking naps, and enjoying fine food. Our packing tips: Bring only the essentials including suntan lotion, beach blanket, sunglasses, Walker's shortbread cookies (a mutual favorite snack), and required reading material: *Gift of the Sea* by Anne Morrow Lindberg.

We agreed to heed Lindberg's words: "One learns first of all in beach living the art of shedding—clothes, vanity, shelter, hypocrisy in human relationships.... Shed the mask and learn how little we can get along with." We also adopted her words as our motto for the week: "How beautiful it is to do nothing. Then to rest afterwards..." We practiced "living in the moment," and we didn't dwell on my failed marriage as a topic of conversation.

~~~

When I returned to New Jersey after a relaxing week with Noelle, I found out that Victor's parents had arrived from Florida for a visit. Marion, Victor's mother, scheduled an entire day for "us two girls" to spend together, rehashing the demise of my marriage with Victor. She was appalled at my weight loss and gave me all kinds of advice to fatten me up. We later joined Victor's father at my sister-in-law's house and compared notes on how clueless we all had been about Victor's same-gender inclinations.

What about the notion that "mothers always know when their son is gay"? Marion never said anything to me about having or denying such omniscient insight; she seemed equally mystified or at least too polite to admit any doubts about Victor's sexual orientation to me, her daughter-in-law.

Both of Victor's parents seemed to be making the best of things, being accepting of Victor but not his new lifestyle. They wanted to stay in touch with me, and I hoped we could still be close because I cared about them. We talked about how relieved I was that Victor had signed the financial agreement that both of our lawyers had reviewed. Our divorce would soon be final.

~~~

In August, Marty, the friend who sang Victor's song at our wedding, invited me to attend a Saturday night party in Massachusetts. Nathan agreed to come with me. But my regular pet sitter wasn't available so I decided to check with Victor; he agreed to take care of Champ and Clover for the weekend, much to my surprise. He still had a key to the house and promised he would stop by on Saturday while we were gone. The plan was to return Champ to my house on Sunday morning so he and Howard could make other plans for the rest of Sunday.

Nathan and I made the trip to Massachusetts, had a great visit spending time with Marty and his family, and started back to New Jersey early Sunday morning. I had a new habit of waking up "with the morning birds." Nathan was an early riser as well. We arrived back to my house by one o'clock in the afternoon. I saw Victor's car in my driveway.

"Well, it looks like you'll have the opportunity to meet Victor today, if you like," I said to Nathan as we parked along the curb. "He must be here dropping off Champ. I'm sure he won't be sticking around long."

"That's okay with me. Do you think Victor's here alone?"

"He better be here alone. He most certainly knows I don't want Howard anywhere near this house."

We jumped out of my car and approached the front door. I rang the doorbell before unlocking the door and shouted out, "I'm home," as I walked down the hallway to the kitchen and family room.

"You're home early," said Victor, as he walked out of the family room to meet me in the kitchen. "How was your trip?"

"It went very well, thank you. Victor, I want to introduce you to my friend Nathan. Nathan, this is Victor."

They shook hands.

"Oh, Howard's here, too," said Victor, pointing to the family room. "We're here doing our laundry."

I glanced in the family room. There he was—Mr. Evil Incarnate—sitting on the loveseat.

"What? No, don't tell me this. Victor, this is so awkward. Please come into the dining room with me."

We stepped into the dining room.

I felt betrayed. I had made it clear to Victor that he was not allowed to bring Howard into my home. I had trusted Victor to respect my privacy. He had violated my boundary. Nathan was an invited guest, but Howard was no guest of mine.

"Victor, get the hell out of this house right now." I screamed in a hushed voice, emphatically. "How dare you bring that man in this house! You are sitting here watching your monster TV together and doing your laundry in my house? You have some nerve."

"Hey, calm down," said Victor. "We're just doing our laundry. It's such a pain to go to the laundromat."

"No, you've just hit a new all-time low. I'm so angry at you. Get out of here. Now. This very minute."

"What about our laundry?" Victor said.

"I don't care about your laundry. Get out of here now. If I calm down, you can come back—alone—after six o'clock and pick up your precious laundry. And don't forget to bring your house key and any copies you have. That's it. I can no longer trust you. Ever."

"Gee, Vivian, I'm sorry. I had no idea you would be so upset."

I believed he was sorry about getting caught more than he was sorry about going against my will; he had turned into a man I could no longer trust.

"End of conversation," I declared. "Get out, now!"

Victor and Howard scrambled out the door in a hurry, leaving their wet laundry behind on the spin cycle.

~~~

Anger was something I rarely felt or expressed. I have always felt uncomfortable being around anyone who is angry and will do whatever I can to avoid confrontations that will lead to people becoming angry at me. I understood that failure to feel and express anger made me vulnerable to becoming a doormat to others, allowing people to walk all over me and take advantage of me. And I hated the feeling of being used; I was no stranger to the hurt feelings and the humiliation that accompany this feeling. But when someone I love violates clear boundaries we both agreed to respect, I explode inside with anger.

Nathan tried to calm me down after they left, but I was livid. I never even wanted Howard or any of Victor's new friends to know my address, let alone come inside where I lived. I could picture them getting drunk, having a fight, and then someone deciding to get back at Victor by doing something bad to me. I wanted to buy a gun—for self-defense. They were trespassers. My house felt so violated. *Forgive our trespasses as we forgive those who trespass against us?* No way! Victor went way over the line on this one. Never again would I ask him to take care of Champ and Clover. I was as mad as I could possibly be at him. I despised him for bringing Howard into my house.

Chapter 27

It was a personal victory that I was finally able to unleash my anger toward Victor after I saw Howard in my house. However, I decided not to languish in my anger state. I didn't have that kind of time and energy to waste on anger. I was busy trying to rebuild my life.

I had a business trip to Washington, DC, with my boss, Katarina, on Monday and my annual one-on-one meeting with the Foundation's President on Tuesday—both of these scheduled commitments went well. And then Nathan invited me to celebrate my 37th birthday with a three-day trip to the White Mountains of New Hampshire at the end of the week. We had a fun time being together, staying in a cabin, reading books, and exploring the wonders of nature in the surrounding area. We pondered the local sights, including the Old Man in the Mountain and the Flume. We also visited The Frost Place, which celebrates the poetry of Robert Frost with a half-mile Poetry Nature Trail. We walked through fields and woods on this trail, meandering among Frost's poems that were mounted on plaques in the midst of dozens of New England wildflowers and plants. My relationship with Nathan helped restore my sense of self-worth and my faith in the power of love. We had a marvelous time together and then made the long drive back to New Jersey.

~~~

September was full of interesting work assignments and travel, including making presentations to groups of grantseekers, fundraisers, and communications professionals and attending conferences in San Francisco, Baltimore, and Chicago.

Of special note was a fabulous experience in San Francisco, being part of a conference for the Foundation's extended family of communications professionals throughout the country in which Katarina had taken the leadership role to orchestrate. The camaraderie was exquisite, both in terms of professional growth and developing friendships with competent individuals who attended this conference. I was lucky enough to experience the best haircut of my life at a salon in downtown San Francisco. I took excursions to Muir Woods and a wine country tour with colleagues. I was especially pleased to find a gift to bring back to New Jersey for Nathan—a colorful, handcrafted carving of an armadillo, which had a special meaning to him comparable to my passion for rabbits. At the tail end of the conference in San Francisco, Katarina received the official word: The Foundation's President had hired a new Vice President for our communications office named Simon Hamilton, who would come on board within the next few months.

~~~

One day during September I had a flat tire—a blowout on the front passenger's side of my car—on my way to work. Fortunately, I was traveling through a residential area and managed to pull the car off the road into a school parking lot. I had serious doubts about having enough physical strength to change a flat. Yet, I proceeded one step at a time, first loosening the lug nuts with the wrench, then tugging my way to make the car jack work, removing the flat tire and replacing it with the spare, and then tightening the lug nuts secure enough to travel safely. I felt like the Little Engine That Could, muttering to myself, *I think I can, I think I can* as I performed each task. I was overjoyed with a new sense of accomplishment that I could do this on my own! When I arrived at work, everyone was impressed that I could pull this off—evidence of a vast improvement in the health of my body, compared to four months earlier. I was starting to feel like a strong woman.

~~~

I was eager to share my saga of the flat tire success story with Nathan, as well as relay all of my recent work-related adventures and give him the armadillo carving, during our Tuesday night of watching boxing on television together at my place. Nathan was back in the classroom teaching high school students, so he had plenty of stories to share with me as well.

After a bit of small talk I asked him if he wanted some dinner.

"No, thanks. I'm stuffed. I just ate way too much. Julie made me a fantastic supper after school today."

"Oh? Who's Julie?"

"Julie is my wife."

I froze, dumbfounded.

"Nathan, you have a wife?"

"Yes, I do."

"Where does Julie live?"

"She lives at my house. I guess I should say at our house."

"Wait a minute. Nathan, you're married? How come you never told me that?"

"Well, you never asked."

He spoke in a matter-of-fact manner, seemingly oblivious to the devastating impact of this revelation on me.

"What do you mean, I never asked? It's my responsibility to ask you if you're married?"

"I've never lied to you," he said. "And besides, it's hardly a marriage. We don't sleep in the same bed. I've been sleeping on the couch for years now."

"Nathan, it's none of my business where you sleep. But I can't believe you never told me that you're married. I certainly have no business being involved with a married man."

"Well, you're technically married, right?"

"I've been totally transparent with you about Victor from day one of our relationship, telling you much more than you probably ever want to know about me and my marriage to Victor."

"So, what's the big deal? I'm in love with you, not Julie."

"You're in love with me? Come on, Nathan. Don't give me that line."

"But it's the truth. I've never been so happy since you came into my life."

"This just won't work. Don't you understand? I can't spend time with you when you have a wife. You mean, you let your wife cook you a great meal and then come over to see me? What a scumbag! That's totally unacceptable. How can you do that?"

"She's a teacher, too, and our schedules work out so we sometimes have supper at the same time after school."

The more he tried to rationalize his actions, the more frustrated I became.

"Listen, you just don't get it. A woman doesn't do this to another woman. It's against everything I believe in, including the sisterhood of women. Women need to empower and lift one another up, not bring each other down and destroy marriages in the process. If you have problems in your marriage, you need to be home working things out, not here with me. How could you do this to me?"

"Okay, so you're upset. But that doesn't change how I feel about you, Vivian."

"Well, it changes everything for me. First of all, infidelity is just plain wrong. Period. We're breaking the commandment about 'thou shalt not commit adultery' without me even knowing about it. I feel like such an idiot. Furthermore, I think there are some legal issues here, including alienation of affection. Julie could come after me using a crime of passion defense. You own a gun, don't you?"

"Oh, don't worry about that. She doesn't care that much about me to come after you."

"I don't know that. Never underestimate the wrath of a woman scorned—"

"Really, it's not like that."

"Does Julie know anything about me or us?"

"Of course not. She knows nothing."

"Well, you know what all this makes me?"

"What do you mean, Vivian?"

"A mistress. And that's the polite term. I can't believe it. How could you do this to me? And how could this happen to me?"

"Vivian, I never planned any of this. It just happened. And I love being with you."

"Well, this is a no-win situation for me. We need to stop seeing each other. Now."

"No, don't do this to me," said Nathan.

"Hey, this is pretty overwhelming for me to take in all at once. I think you better leave now."

"Really? Are you serious?"

"You better believe I'm serious. Go home and watch boxing with Julie."

"Okay, so you need some time to think things over and come to your senses. I'm a patient man. I'll be here for you when you want me back."

"Good-bye, Nathan." I felt the need to slam doors and smash glass but instead regained my composure enough to escort Nathan out of my house and out of my life.

"Good night, Vivian," he said as he left with his armadillo gift in hand.

I was both angry and sad when I closed the door on Nathan. His dishonesty was a major disappointment, but I knew I would miss him and his friendship.

Later that evening, I took a long, hard look at myself in the mirror. I felt like such a fool. First, I married a man who turned out to be gay. Then I became involved with a man who turned out to be married.

I studied every feature on my face. I zeroed in on a mole located about an inch from the left corner of my mouth. Nathan often told me how much he adored that beauty mark, as if it was one feature I shared with Marilyn Monroe. He would lovingly trace his finger around this spot, even making some sort of poetic expressions about its shape and texture. Frankly, I never gave it much thought, thinking it was something to cover up with some makeup.

On an impulse, I started to manipulate this mole with my fingers, trying all sorts of ways to figure out how I could rip it off. Each day I worked on removing this mole with my fingers, making it bleed and scab over. At some point I convinced myself that this was some sort of self-flagellation— perhaps it was my personal badge of shame as a punishment for my lack of judgment about Nathan and a way to inflict pain on myself as a test to endure such small-scale physical torture. I later rationalized my self-mutilation as a permanent reminder of Nathan's deception, making sure that never again would I allow someone to define that mole on my face as a beauty mark.

Chapter 28

Coming to terms with the abrupt ending of my short-lived romance with Nathan was a matter of mind over feelings. Everything about Nathan that I found so appealing—the way he gave me his full attention, his charm, his wit, his sense of humor, his companionship, his ability to lift my spirits, and his deep, low register voice—was canceled out by the overriding reality that he was a married man. I didn't fall apart over his self-revelation; I took the necessary corrective action of dismissing him from my life. Deconstructing the meaning of Nathan and how he touched my life was fodder for self-learning in my work with Dr. Barley, who provided expert guidance on letting go of this no-win relationship.

Nathan didn't disappear from my life; he called me, left messages on my answering machine, and sent me letters, poems, and cards—even flower bouquets on occasion. But I was adamant about no longer seeing him, knowing how easily I could cave in to being "in the moment" with him. Our friendship could only be a fond memory for me.

I kept my focus on my work, as well as taking care of myself by eating well. I was allowed to resume my workouts in the fitness center, as long as I was sensible about it, and ride my bike on the weekends. Moving my body through exercise really helped me keep my balance. I spent my leisure time reading and writing, as well as enjoying Champ and Clover. I also joined a women's book club.

I decided to attend the wedding of a coworker of Victor's when I learned Victor would be going alone, knowing that he would be on his best behavior in the midst of his workplace colleagues. I was happy for this young couple, who Victor and I had spent time with during the past couple of years; it was a happy event. Although we arrived in separate cars, Victor and I were seated at the same table at the wedding reception and had enjoyable conversations about the wedding, including joining the celebration for a few songs on the dance floor. On the way home, we stopped off for coffee at a diner. We agreed to relate to one another as good friends, not soon-to-be-divorced partners. It was no longer unbearably painful for me to spend time with Victor, as long as he kept details about his love life to himself.

~~~

The following week I traveled to Scottsdale, Arizona, to attend a conference for communications professionals in the foundation world. I extended my stay in Arizona for a couple of extra days so I could meet up with my best friend from high school, who had moved out there with her husband. I hadn't seen her for 15 years. She was my matron of honor, but we had only kept in touch through our sporadic letters. She was happily married and now had two daughters, 13 and 11 years of age, whom I had never met. It was a great reunion, and we talked nonstop for the entire two days of my visit before I returned back home to New Jersey. This visit reminded me how nice it is to spend time with a close girlfriend, something I never bothered to cultivate once Victor came into my life.

~~~

One night, 10 months after Victor moved out and three months after I had unleashed my anger at him when he had brought Howard into my house to do their laundry, I received a telephone call late at night.

"Hello?"

"Hi, it's me," said Victor.

"Oh, Victor. How are you?"

"Not so good."

"What's wrong?"

"Well, it's a bad scene here with Howard."

"Trouble in paradise?" I asked, as I heard ice cubes jiggling together in a glass on the other end of the telephone.

"Vivian, I really miss my old life. With you. Life can be so hard and cold and cruel. I want my old life back."

Over the past few weeks, Dr. Barley had prepared me for the possibility that Victor might reconsider his options and even try to get back together with me. I found that hard to believe and dismissed that possibility. But Dr. Barley insisted that we role-play such a scenario, which helped me come up with a response without hesitation.

"That's too bad, Victor. I'm so sorry to hear that."

"It's not any fun anymore. And it's no fun living with someone with a serious drinking problem."

"Oh, really?"

"Yes, really."

Dr. Barley had cautioned me about the importance of staying true to my boundaries with Victor. No flip-flops in our relationship were allowed. I was starting to recover from the cataclysmic fallout of Victor's decision to move out 10 months ago, and I still had a long way to go to build a strong, healthy, and unshakable sense of self. I needed to do whatever it would take to avoid any more setbacks. Becoming any more entangled with Victor could trigger some sort of toxic effect. As Dr. Barley confided in me, "You've worked so hard. But you don't have another round in you when it comes to Victor." I believed Dr. Barley was right about that.

I had also learned that self-esteem was like a muscle that needed to be built up, strengthened, and flexed on an ongoing basis. I couldn't let anything interfere with taking care of myself, which also included taking care of my feelings.

"Victor, I'm not sure exactly what you're saying. But you know you can never have your old life back here with me. There's no turning back."

"Are you sure?"

"Oh, yes. I'm sure."

"Well, at the very least, can you help me figure out what to do about Howard?"

"No, I can't give you any advice on your love life."

"Well, how about some advice on living with someone with a drinking problem? I know you've read all those books on being a codependent. You even went to some kind of AA meeting for codependents, right?"

"Victor, everything I tried to do to help you with your drinking problem didn't work, remember? It's up to the person with a drinking problem to admit there's a problem and then to do something about it."

"Well, I guess you're right. But this is really hard. I don't like it one bit. It's really depressing."

"Victor, after all I've gone through during the last 10 months, I really can't believe you're at a point where you miss your old life. Remember how miserable you said you were with me? Remember the daily torture of having strong same-gender feelings?"

"Yeah. I know I've come a long way. But I didn't know things would turn out like this."

"Victor, I'm really not the one to help you now. You need to find help from someone else."

"Okay, I just thought I would give it a try with you. I miss you."

"Okay, good night now."

"Good night, Vivian."

I wanted Victor to find happiness in his new life so I felt sorry about his disillusionment with Howard. At the same time I felt strong and capable about the way I had handled his call. I knew we could never go back to the life we left behind.

~~~

After Victor's phone call, I became even more absorbed in my work. Trying to become conversant about the ever-changing landscape of health policy and its myriad, mind-boggling intricacies was a challenge. Always on the lookout for interesting ways to communicate the practical implications of health issues, I focused on collecting success stories that grantees and health advocates had developed to attract media interest.

For example, I was intrigued by the work of others in using a social math approach to help people understand the prevalence of binge drinking among college students. Instead of stating that American college students consume 430 gallons of alcohol each year, there's a better way to grab people's attention. As researcher Lawrence Wallack wrote in 1993, "enough alcohol (was) consumed by college students (in a year) to fill 3,500 Olympic-size swimming pools, about one on every campus in the United States"—this statement has more impact and is more memorable for the general public. This image of a swimming pool full of alcohol has come to mind whenever I visit any college campus.

I decided to reach out to various publications to pitch story ideas on topics I felt needed more attention, while at the same time building relationships with magazine editors who may be interested in using me as a contributing freelance writer for feature articles. My supervisor, Katarina, was supportive to my interest in exploring the possibilities of writing for other publications.

I contacted a local magazine publisher I had crossed paths with at a conference and made a story pitch in a letter to him. He responded by inviting me to stop by his office. When I showed up, he introduced me to the editor of his magazine, who turned out to be a tall, good-looking man named Christopher Drake. We greeted one another with a cordial handshake, but then I felt self-conscious for a moment when I saw him glance at my left hand. I wondered whether he was checking to see if I was wearing a wedding ring.

"I understand you want to do some freelance writing for our magazine," he said.

"That's right. I have a ton of story ideas that I believe your readers would find quite interesting."

"Well, I see you have sent us a 1,000-word writing sample, based on some of the lessons learned in your work in the foundation world. I'm working on deadline now for our next issue so I haven't had a chance to read it yet."

"On deadline? In that case, let me get out of your way," I said.

We agreed to meet over lunch the following Friday, away from all the distractions at work.

~~~

When we met at a nearby restaurant that Friday, I was in a bubbly mood, eager to talk about the recent feature stories I had found interesting in his magazine as well as my story ideas. Christopher seemed interested in me and my work, posing typical questions that a reporter would ask about my background and writing experience. I, in turn, told him I was curious about his work as a magazine editor. He shared a few stories about the trials and tribulations of working in the magazine world, and I shared a few stories about my passion for working with grantees and colleagues in the foundation world. At one point in the conversation I reached over, without giving it much thought, and placed my hand on the back of his hand, which was resting on the table, to make a point. Christopher remained motionless, staring at my hand on his hand, and then made direct eye contact with me. I stopped talking. Then, he broke into a warm smile.

"Oh, am I invading your personal space?" I said as I removed my hand from the table. "Sometimes I talk with my hands. Really, I'm not one of those touchy-feely people. I guess I just got carried away, too wrapped up in the story I'm telling."

"That's okay. I don't mind," he said.

"I think you're right about talking over lunch away from the office. It's much more relaxing without any work interruptions."

"Yes, it's good to get away from my desk and all the piles of work."

"So, what about my story ideas? Any chance you can use me to write for your magazine?"

"Oh, I think that's a possibility. I've got another idea. How about we consider the work part of this lunch over and talk about our personal lives?"

"Well, what do you want to know?" I asked. I felt flattered by his attention.

"Anything you feel like telling me."

"Let's see. I'll try giving you the short version, not the long-winded saga. I live alone, with my dog, Champ, and my house rabbit, Clover. No husband—he moved out 11 months ago—and no children. No significant other in my life now. How about you? Are you married?"

"No, no more wife. We're divorced. But I have two great sons, now ages nine and 11. Joint custody. No serious girlfriend."

"Well, I'm not exactly shopping for a man these days. I'm still trying to pull myself together. It's been a real struggle for me so far. But I'm always on the lookout for someone who wants to be my friend."

"Bingo. Consider me friend material. How about letting me, your new friend, take you out to dinner?"

"Really? You mean, a date?"

"If that's what you want to call it," he said with a smile.

I had mixed feelings about his intentions but decided to give him the benefit of the doubt. He was a tall, good-looking man, someone I wanted to get to know better.

"Sure, I would love to go out for dinner with you."

"How about this Sunday? At 6:00 p.m.?"

"Yes. I'll give you directions to my place."

~~~

I was somewhat nervous about going out on my first official date with Christopher. I didn't know diddly-squat about what to do and what not to do on a first date. I was certain the dating scene had changed in the past 20 years, when I first became involved with Victor. Furthermore, although I was no longer a 19-year-old wallflower, I was clueless about expectations between two adults who had just met one another. It was too late to write a letter to Dear Abby or look up any relevant articles in my back issues of *Self* magazine; I had always skipped over any articles on the topic of dating etiquette. I was too bashful and embarrassed to ask for candid advice from any of my female friends or my sisters or my mother or even my therapist. And, for obvious reasons, it was out of the question to contact Victor or Nathan about this.

What I did know I had to do was this: (1) find out if he's gay and (2) find out if he's married. Beyond that, I would have to improvise.

Chapter 29

Christopher and I hit it off from the moment he arrived to pick me up on Sunday night. I introduced him to Champ and Clover and gave him a guided tour of my townhome.

"I feel like I'm playing show-and-tell," I said. "But I think you can tell a lot about me by taking a look around here. For example, my pets are important. I would be unbearably lonely without them. I love books, which you see all over the place. I love the piano, but I really only play it for my own amusement. So don't expect any piano recitals from me tonight. And I adore my job, which is the real anchor in my life now."

"Well, that's all very interesting," said Christopher, making direct eye contact with me.

"I guess what I'm saying is I'm a what-you-see-is-what-you-get kind of person." I hoped he was, too—without any disturbing surprises.

Christopher brought me to a local Italian restaurant. After a romantic dinner with stimulating conversation, candlelight, wine, and tiramisu for dessert, I felt at ease with him. He was charming; he came across as an attentive listener and had a great sense of humor.

We both talked about how lonely it was to be single and how difficult it was to even consider the possibility of becoming romantically involved with someone else. Christopher talked about the despair of being betrayed, which prompted me to mention seeing the movie, *They Shoot Horses, Don't They?* We confided that at times we both had felt as if we should be put out of our misery, but then we lightened up with banter about our not being cut out to dance the Lindy in a marathon dance competition. Nevertheless, we both had trust issues. And we both felt awkward about dating.

It was still early when Christopher drove me home in his rather beat-up BMW—a remnant from his shattered marriage—that rattled a bit on the back roads leading to my townhome; his former wife ended up with the newer model car, he explained. I was relieved to hear his divorce was final; his wife had dumped him for another man a few years ago.

"It's only eight o'clock. Would you like to come in?" I asked, hoping I could spend more time with him instead of being alone all evening. "I can make a pot of coffee. And perhaps even light up a Duraflame log in the fireplace, if you like."

"Sure. I would like that."

Within minutes, the coffee was brewed. Champ settled down and stretched out on the carpet away from the fireplace. Christopher and I took off our shoes and curled up on the couch in front of the glow of the fireplace, sipping our mugs of coffee as we talked about how we were coping with rejection. It felt really good to be with a man who was treating me so well. His presence filled a void in my life. As far as I could tell, he was definitely heterosexual and not married. Also, he made it clear his boys came first in his life, which made sense to me. I knew I could fall for him in a big way.

Eventually we stopped talking and gazed at each other. Within moments, we kissed. It was pleasant. It felt good. We kissed again.

"Is this okay?" I asked.

"It's okay with me. How about you?"

"It feels great. I really like being with you, Christopher."

"Well, I really like being with you, Vivian."

"Enough to take things a little further?" I said, revealing myself as an affection-starved woman with a hunger for touch growing ever stronger.

"What did you have in mind?"

"I'm thinking I could make you feel real good, if you like," I said, as I reached to unbuckle his belt.

"Things are moving a little fast here, don't you think?"

"Oh, too fast for you?"

"I didn't say too fast. I just said things are moving a little fast."

"I'm improvising. I don't really know what I'm supposed to do or not supposed to do. I just know it feels right to be with you. Do you want me to stop?"

"No, not really," he said with a bashful grin.

"Well, then. Why not? We're both adults. Let's move beyond the awkward stage and see if we're compatible."

"Oh, I have no doubt that we're compatible."

"Let's see. It's more comfortable without having our clothes get in the way," I said, as I started to undress and helped him out of his clothes.

We stayed on the couch as we started to explore each other's body.

"Easy, easy, easy," he said in a gentle yet commanding tone.

His words were the coolant I needed to bring me out of the vapors of passion so I could observe I was making love to a man who enjoys both giving and receiving affection.

I paused to gaze into his face. No, I hadn't inadvertently caused an injury. At worst, I could see a grimace of tolerant discomfort, not pain. But I realized at that moment I was on my way to being too caught up in the motion, imposing a rhythm programmed in my mind years earlier that took no account of playful discovery or elongated tenderness. His eyes told me I was now free of any expectation to master the intricate steps of a prescribed pattern, as one must do when dancing the Lindy.

Synchronized lovemaking, I thought, wondering why I felt the need to come up with a technical term for the splendor I was experiencing. It felt fluid, spontaneous, even haphazard.

With Christopher, I felt a sense of adventure, as if we were taking a journey that didn't require a map or even a destination. We were secure in feeling the magic of being together, skin to skin, both craving connection.

~~~

The next morning I woke up in my bed, with Champ at my side. *Was that just a really nice dream I had last night?* I wondered. But I realized it was all true: Ashes from the Duraflame log were in the fireplace, two empty mugs were on the coffee table, and leftovers from my dinner out were in a doggie bag in my refrigerator. Christopher did not stay overnight, as we both had to get to work early on Monday morning. Yet when I went to my front door to retrieve my morning newspaper, I found a single, long-stemmed, salmon-colored rose on my doorstep. Christopher must have delivered it on his way to work that morning. I was thrilled by his romantic gesture.

But I was also worried about what came next. Was I supposed to call and thank him for a fabulous dinner? Or was he supposed to call and thank me for a spectacular evening?

Luckily, I didn't have to worry long. Christopher called me later that day. We agreed to meet again on Tuesday evening at my place.

~~~

On Tuesday he arrived at my front door with a long-stemmed red rose for me.

"This one is to keep the salmon-colored rose company so it won't be lonely," he said.

So we placed the two roses in the same vase, noting that the salmon-colored rose was now in full bloom.

We spent the evening together, talking and getting to know one another better. It was clear to both of us we had stumbled upon something extraordinary—namely, each other. We agreed our relationship was off to a great start.

We continued to see each other whenever possible. I took my diaphragm out of storage from the days before Victor's vasectomy to discover cobwebs—not a good sign. Also it was probably no longer a correct fit due to my weight loss. So I made it a priority to see my doctor for effective contraception right away. I had never had unprotected sex in my life, and reliable birth control was imperative.

I was filled with joyous wonder to have Christopher in my life. I was so moved I actually jotted down these words in my journal:

> This passion-filled whirlwind—a tornado of romance—blows apart my pedestrian notions of growing close to a man. With missionary zeal, his self-appointed crusade to show me unrestrained pleasure—enveloped in genuine caring—has taken hold. Many women go through entire lifetimes without peak experiences, while I discover a lifetime of peak experiences in a single evening. I am truly amazed and grateful.

> Now, with this love artist in my life, I treasure these days—the skyrocket excitement, the libido-quenching contentment, the energizing stamina, the healing power of his touch.

Without a doubt, nothing made me feel more alive than being loved.

Chapter 30

Nearly two months later on New Year's Eve 1993, I was home alone with Champ and Clover, taking stock of all the changes in my life during the past year.

First of all, I was still alive. With lots of hard work, I had managed to inch my way back to a normal weight and not slip backwards; my days of "situational anorexia" were history. I had learned to stop the food deprivation habits that drove my health into the dark abyss soon after Victor moved out.

I realized I almost didn't survive the breakup of my marriage. I not only lost Victor but I also lost the person I was in my marriage to Victor. Such rejection made me feel irreparably punctured like the Hindenburg airship. I vowed to never again allow myself to become so attached and dependent on someone else.

I had managed to hang onto my job. In fact, I was thriving at work. Every day was an adventure. At times I felt I could hardly keep up with the avalanche of developments—it seemed as if everyone around me was constantly working in high gear. But I knew I was holding my own, thanks to the supportive relationship I had with Katarina and the congenial tone she set among our immediate and national fleet of communications professionals. Simon Hamilton, our new Vice President of Communications, was undertaking a herculean vision for the role of communications in the Foundation's work. I wasn't quite sure where I would fit in, but I was eager to move forward under his leadership. I could sense he was destined to make a big splash; I had never encountered a person at his level who showed such an unbridled drive to transform the work of the Foundation for higher visibility and impact. He was going to make history, and I was part of the team. One of the first actions he took was to enroll all of his staff in an Evelyn Wood Speed Reading Workshop, a signal that high-volume workloads were on their way.

In my personal life, I understood making the transition from married to single would require a great deal of imagination. For example, I tried to maintain some friendships that were not dependent on Victor's participation, such as when my neighbor Alice invited me to join her family for Thanksgiving dinner. This time I was the one who made a pumpkin bread to share, and Alice didn't mind that I, as a strict vegetarian, wouldn't eat her turkey or gravy; she was grateful I was still alive and kicking.

I'm living in the present, not the past nor the future, I declared, warding off any mention of Victor over dinner with Alice's family. Instead, I spent the bulk of my Thanksgiving holiday ironing every piece of clothing in my closet while watching 20 hours of work-related management seminars on videotapes about the nursing shortage in America. I pondered if the act of ironing could have any therapeutic value—rolling a high-temperature, electric-powered contraption back and forth over the folds and wrinkles of my pleated skirts and tailored blouses as the iron hissed and the plumes of steam encircled me.

Furthermore, it didn't feel right to try to carry on with all the family holiday traditions as a solo act. So I discarded most of them: no holiday decorations, no Christmas tree, no New Year's Day Open House.

I needed new friends, preferably well-adjusted people who were not self-centered, and scouted around for single women who enjoy being single. I turned to self-help books for guidance but found slim pickings. *The Joy of Being Single* by Allia Zobel was a novelty book of less than 100 pages—mostly illustrations with sparse text—but it was a start.

A few single women worked at the Foundation, but I felt awkward about presenting myself as "friend" material. I especially didn't want to come across as "needy friend" material. Fortunately, I struck up a friendship with Kate, an upbeat, native New Yorker with a great sense of humor and a background in radio who did some freelance work for the Foundation. Kate was my age, single, and living in a townhome with her treasured companion, Doug the Dog.

Kate and I went to movies, concerts, and lectures together. A well-groomed woman with a flair for fashion, Kate introduced me to her favorite hair stylist and nail salon where I became a regular client. We went shopping together; even though I had a longtime aversion to the glamour scene of malls and boutiques, Kate made shopping fun and always encouraged me to add more color to my wardrobe.

Kate was particular about the men she dated; she set high standards and had an independent spirit in the way she approached everything in her life. I also appreciated she was Jewish, not Christian; that meant she didn't pose any "What would Jesus do?" questions when we were talking through various issues in our lives. We respected each other and got along fine, without making burdensome demands on one another. We both loved doing work for the Foundation and being part of the Foundation's social circle.

My relationship with Christopher was growing stronger over time. Our physical attraction for one another was electric whenever the sparks of passion were ignited, making me feel affirmed as a woman. *Perhaps I don't make men turn gay after all,* I concluded. I came to believe no person possesses the power to change another person's sexual orientation. (Years later, I found comfort in reading about a woman in a similar situation whose aunt told her, "You must have been one helluva woman to keep a gay man interested for so long.") But we were both cautious about placing too much faith in one another. For Christopher, his relationship with his two sons was his top priority. He was concerned about introducing me to his boys, not wanting to impose any more difficult adjustments such as figuring out the impact of "Dad has a girlfriend" on them. Naturally, I deferred to his judgment—

somewhat content with our arrangement to spend time together whenever he wasn't with his boys and our busy work schedules would allow. Besides, I wasn't entirely grounded yet nor ready to think much about my future with him or anyone else.

Christopher called me almost every night—usually late at night, at bedtime. Sometimes these conversations lasted an hour or more. Sometimes I could barely stay awake and would begin to doze. But that never seemed to bother Christopher. I think he found satisfaction in tiring me out. An exhausted girlfriend is a faithful one, he must have reasoned.

So I wasn't surprised when he called after midnight—after he had celebrated New Year's Eve with his boys and sent them off to bed—to wish me a Happy New Year.

"Hello, Vivian. Are you alone?"

"Of course. I'm alone here with Champ, in bed, reading a book. Did you have a good time with your boys tonight?"

"Oh yeah. We ate pizza and played videogames and hung out here at my place."

"I'm glad you and your boys are so close. They're lucky to have such a caring dad."

"But I miss being with you, Vivian."

"I miss you, too."

"I've been thinking. Maybe it's time for the boys to meet you."

"Really? That would be great. What do you have in mind?"

"Well, perhaps the three of us could come over to your house on Sunday afternoon and watch the football game together. You know, keep things real low-key."

"I would love to have you visit. I'll serve some snacks and try not to ask too many stupid questions about the football game."

"We can see how it goes. I've told them I have a new friend."

"Should I be nervous? What if they don't like me?"

"Don't worry. Just be yourself."

"But no physical contact in front of your boys, right?"

"That's right. Let's see if they can get used to the idea of me having a new friend first. I'm not sure how they would handle the idea of me having a girlfriend."

"You're calling the shots on this one. 'Father knows best' and all that."

"I'm not sure about the 'Father knows best' part, but I want to do my best for my boys. It's hard enough they've had to get used to their mother having a boyfriend."

"You can count on me. Champ, Clover, and I promise to be on our good behavior. I've read all children of divorced parents secretly want to believe their mother and father will get back together. So if your boys don't warm up to me right away, I'll understand."

"We'll see what happens."

~~~

I liked Benjamin and Luke, Christopher's two sons, right away and how they related to their father. They came across as bright boys with a keen interest in sports, especially baseball. Somewhat quiet at first yet polite, they were friendly to Champ and Clover, ate the snacks I served, and played cards, Yahtzee, and chess with me. I encouraged them to explore my townhome, counting all the items with a rabbit motif they could spot; this is an icebreaker game I play with all children who visit.

After that visit, I was included in several activities Christopher did with his boys over the coming months. We hiked in the woods together, ate many pizzas together, attended the Cub Scout Pinewood Derby racing events, and hung out at Christopher's apartment playing games, drinking soft drinks, and talking about whatever anyone wanted to discuss.

With Little League season fast approaching, I soon learned my ball throwing and catching skills were far inferior to this clan of baseball enthusiasts. But I did my best to show interest in their activities, attending many baseball games and practice sessions on the weekends when Christopher was coaching the teams his sons played on. They educated me about the batting scores of Barry Bonds and the music of Green Day. Soon I felt "accepted" as a tagalong in most situations with the Drake boys, respectful of Christopher's role as their father and assuming my role as the "nice lady" visitor.

My travel schedule at work really took off in the early months of the year, with business trips to Atlanta, Dallas, Boston, Pittsburgh, San Bernardino, and Washington, DC. But I made it a priority to stay in touch with some of the children in my life, including having visits with my nieces and nephews and serving as a piano accompanist when the older sister of my goddaughter was performing "Zip-A-Dee-Do-Da" in a school talent show. Spending time with children was a great way to practice "living in the moment" and moving beyond the loss of my marriage.

~~~

Just as I was starting to feel some level of confidence about managing the rhythm of my life as a working woman living alone and enjoying my blossoming relationship with Christopher and his boys, another curve ball came my way— something that showed me once again that things are not what they appear to be.

Chapter 31

I was driving my car alongside the lake on my way back to my office on a sunny afternoon in mid-April, observing the 35-mile-per-hour speed limit. I saw a cluster of wild ducks making their way across the two-lane road ahead of me.

I checked my rear-view mirror to see that no one was tailgating my car and applied my brakes so that these webbed pedestrians could complete their crossing. For a split second, I imagined I was smack in the middle of Robert McCloskey's classic children's book *Make Way For Ducklings*, which I had just purchased while on a business trip in Boston over the weekend. But before I could ponder the enchantment of the scene, I heard screeching brakes and the scraping sounds of metal against metal.

Suddenly my blue Toyota Celica was catapulted across the other lane of the road, which was miraculously clear of oncoming traffic. Barely missing a woman who was standing at her mailbox at the end of the driveway, my car came to a jerking stop on her lawn. Stunned for a moment, I looked over my right shoulder and saw a tan-colored van had crashed into a tree on the right side of the road after hitting my car from behind.

I turned my car engine off and climbed out of my car, shaking like a quaking aspen. I looked around and saw the woman at the mailbox coming toward me.

"Are you okay?" she asked.

"I'm a bit shook up. How about you?"

"I saw the whole thing," she said. "That van wasn't paying attention."

We crossed the road for a closer look. The airbag on the driver's side of the Plymouth Voyager had inflated, but I saw no movement from inside the van. Another car passing by stopped, and a man with a cell phone jumped out of his car.

"Is everyone okay?" he asked.

"I'm not sure about the van—," I answered.

The man with the cell phone made his way to the van. He opened the front door of the van, exposing a woman hunched over the airbag, moaning.

"Are you hurt?" he asked her.

She did not respond.

"I'll call 9-1-1 and get some help," he said.

While he dialed, the woman began crying out, "I can't see! I can't see!"

"Don't move," said the man with the cell phone. "Stay still until the ambulance comes."

But the woman climbed out of the van, crumpled into a heap on the ground, and began rocking back and forth, screaming, "I can't see! I can't see!"

Just then the man noticed a pair of glasses on the front seat and handed them to the woman. She put on the glasses and continued rocking back and forth.

That's when I realized that she had first dibs on being hysterical about the circumstances. I would need to remain calm.

A police officer and rescue squad soon appeared on the scene. Then the injured woman's husband arrived, with children in his car. It turned out this woman lived in the neighborhood and had just driven home from a trip to Pennsylvania. Thank God the children weren't with her at the time of the crash.

After a police report was filed and the rescue squad had attended to the driver of the van and whisked her off to the hospital, I was left to deal with my car. An auto body shop was located up the road within a couple of miles, and the police officer told me he thought I could make it on my own to the shop if I drove slowly, with him giving me a police escort.

I left my car at the auto body shop, hitched a ride back to my office from the mechanic, and made arrangements over the telephone for a rental car, which I could pick up the next morning. However, that left me without a way home later that day, a one-hour commute.

I quickly came up with a narrative to assure Katarina and other coworkers I was calm and in control.

"So, the van driver was hurt and received a summons for inattentive driving, the van was crushed, the tree was bruised, and my car is probably going to be declared a total loss, according to the body shop. But the waterfowl are fine. And I escaped with no physical injuries. All in all, I consider myself a lucky duck."

They were relieved I was okay, and everyone returned to our business-as-usual rhythm of the day.

All I needed to do was to call Christopher at work and ask him to give me a ride home. My office was only a 10-minute drive from his office; I had given him many rides to and from work when his car needed repairs, including helping him out when his car broke down and using my Triple A card for towing his car to the repair shop of his choice.

"Christopher, it's me."

"Oh, hi. What a surprise to hear from you in the middle of the day."

"Listen, I'm okay, but I just had a serious car accident. My car is at the body shop, and I'm back at work now. Can you give me a ride home tonight?"

Silence.

"Christopher, are you there? Can you give me a ride home tonight?"

"I don't know."

"What do you mean?"

"I really don't know if I can do that for you."

Wrong answer, I thought to myself. I was stunned by his hesitation. I found his reaction more upsetting than the experience of having my car accident.

"I don't understand. I know it's Monday night, your night with your boys. But all I'm asking is for you to stop by and pick me up on your way home. I can leave any time that works for you. I'll meet you right at the front entrance."

Silence again.

"Christopher, what's the big deal? I need your help. I've just had a serious car accident. You're my boyfriend, and I'm your girlfriend. Aren't we supposed to be there for each other when bad things happen? This is certainly one of those times."

"Vivian, it means I have to make a phone call."

"Yeah, well? Do your boys need a ride for something going on with them tonight?"

"No, nothing like that. But they expect me at a certain time. I don't like to deviate from our routine. And it's uncomfortable for me to change my plans."

"Uncomfortable for you? I've just had a serious car accident. I'm lucky to be alive and not in the hospital right now. I'm asking you for a ride home. I don't know what I can do if you don't help me. I guess my choices are to call Victor or Nathan. There's a good chance either one of them will stop whatever they're doing and make it a priority to help me in case of an emergency, even if it means a two-hour roundtrip for them. Is that what you want me to do?"

"Okay. I'll see what I can do."

~~~

I was devastated. What was the point of having Christopher in my life if he couldn't help me in a time of crisis? Our relationship was a two-way street, right? If I couldn't depend on him, who could I depend upon, I wondered. In fact, why bother having a man in my life at all?

My emotions welled up; I was a volcano ready to erupt. I tried to coach myself to remain calm, but I was overwhelmed. I felt all alone in the world. I couldn't think straight. I decided to call my therapist, which was one of the rare times I resorted to making a crisis intervention call to him.

"Dr. Barley, I'm okay but I got into a serious car accident today. I have no car now. And when I called Christopher for a ride home, he said he didn't know if he could help me. I'm so hurt and upset." And then I burst into convulsive crying.

"Vivian, where are you now?"

"I'm here at work. Really, I'm safe and sound. I don't want to make a scene here. And I'm so sorry to bother you with this. I just need you to talk me down and help me get a grip on this. I've handled the car accident just fine, and I made arrangements for getting a rental car tomorrow. But Christopher has really thrown me for a loop just now."

"Take a deep breath, Vivian. Of course you're upset. Let's back up and talk this through."

So we did talk it through. Dr. Barley asked me what I would do if someone I cared about asked me for a ride home after having a serious car accident. In other words, what if Christopher was the one asking me for a ride?

"That's a no-brainer. I would say 'yes' right away and then figure out how to make it happen," I explained.

"Okay. So now you know what a reasonable response would be."

"So what do I do now? I guess that means I have to call Victor or Nathan to see if they can help me. But I know it's not a good idea for me to have any contact with either of them."

Just then I saw that Christopher was calling on the other line; my secretary had put him on hold. I ended the call with Dr. Barley, thinking perhaps Christopher had come to his senses, and took the call.

~~~

Christopher did give me a ride home, telling me he had made arrangements to switch his night with his boys to the next night. And he offered to give me a ride the next morning to pick up my rental car. But I wasn't happy. I decided not to make a big deal about it; after all, he did pick me up and bring me home. I didn't want to spend the ride home complaining about his egregious reaction to my request for a ride. I thanked him for the ride, but told him I was too exhausted and emotionally drained to spend time with him that night.

The truth was he had just toppled off the pedestal I had him on, but I had no energy to confront him about it. Perhaps he was teaching me a lesson about not taking him for granted? Or maybe he saw this as an opportunity to make it clear his boys came first, no matter what, even in case of an emergency? Or maybe I was overreacting? Whatever the reason, I coached myself to be careful and not put too much trust in this relationship. While I was intrigued by the possibility of a future with Christopher and his boys, I felt the beginnings of doubt and insecurity.

~~~

As it turned out, my car insurance agent did declare my car a total loss; the undercarriage of the car was damaged beyond repair. I later received a check for $3,000.

I had never bought a car before; Victor was the one who knew how to shop for a car. I hardly knew where to start. But people at work were willing to offer their advice. Both the Foundation's President and my friend Kate had bought Saturn cars from a dealer near my office. And they both had satisfying experiences there. Kate told me the guys in the service department were really friendly and cute and fun to flirt with—and they took good care of all the maintenance needs of her car.

I mustered up the courage to visit this dealership one day after work. I walked into the showroom and was greeted by a sales representative who was low-key but eager to help. He showed me some cars, and I took a test drive. No haggling over the price; one sticker price was on display. I learned I could save $1,000 by buying a four-door, instead of a two-door, model. Then I learned I could save another $1,000 by buying a car with a manual, not an automatic, transmission. Since I could easily manage a stick shift from my Jeep-driving days, I chose this cost-saving option. I signed the paperwork and was given fresh roses by the sales representative to seal the deal.

Within a week, my car was ready for pickup—complete with the joyous sound of "Banzai! Banzai! Banzai!" from a large group of Saturn employees who cheered me on as I drove my brand-new, golden, 1994 Saturn off the showroom floor and onto the bustling freeway. I did it! I bought a car of my own, all by myself.

A week later, I received a huge box at my doorstep that contained inflated hot air balloons and fresh-baked cookies with a "Welcome to the Saturn Family!" note card. Those added touches really made me feel special. I discovered buying a car can be a celebration, not an anxiety-riddled, dreaded chore. Bouncing back yet again, I was ready to hit the road with a new sense of adventure.

Chapter 32

A few weeks later, in the middle of a routine workday, my new secretary, Ava, walked into my office with a message: "Simon wants you to meet him in his office right away."

I took a brief look in my mirror to make sure my hair looked presentable, grabbed my notebook and pen, and walked briskly to Simon's office, expecting a new assignment. Simon greeted me, asked me to take a seat on his leather couch, and shut the door of his office before he sat down in his high-back executive chair.

"Vivian, I have big plans for my work here as Vice President," said Simon. "Unfortunately, you're not part of my plans. So I'm letting you go."

"Oh, no," I said, feeling myself sinking into the sludge of corporate quicksand. "You mean I don't have a job here anymore?"

"That's right. Starting now, I want to remove you from any projects you have on your plate. Instead, your only responsibility will be to find a new job."

I was stunned. I took a deep breath and tried to collect my thoughts. Perhaps I could try to reason with Simon? I decided to give it a try.

"I understand it's your prerogative to handpick your own team, and I'm a leftover from the previous Vice President," I said. "Perhaps I could transfer to another job here at the Foundation? For example, I know we're expanding our library."

"No, that's out of the question. We're going through a major reorganization here, and people are looking at me to make staff changes. You will no longer be able to work here."

"Well, this comes as quite a shock to me," I stammered. "I've been working here for almost five years. The Foundation has invested a lot in me. I'm deeply committed to the mission and work of this organization. In fact, the people here have become my family."

"Listen, I know you're regarded as a good worker, and you are well-liked by your coworkers. I can provide references for you. I know it takes time to find a new job, especially if you want to stay in the foundation world. So you can come and go as you please here at the office for the next few months. And you can call upon our new secretary, Ava, to provide administrative support to you in your job search, although her primary job now will be to work for Janet. Furthermore, I'll make sure we pay for any job search–related expenses for domestic travel to meet and network with other foundations. But you are removed from any strategy building activities of my team."

I listened to his words, but they were barely sinking in. He made it clear that there was no room for negotiation. I mustered up my courage to ask a direct question.

"What did I do wrong, Simon?"

"It's not a matter of doing anything wrong," he said, shifting in his chair and glancing at his appointment book. "I just don't want you on my team moving forward."

I paused, trying to absorb his candor. I could see he had already tossed me in his discard pile.

"So how do you want me to handle sharing this news with others?" I asked.

"Well, Katarina already knows about this, as well as the Foundation's President. You can tell anyone whatever you want about your plans to leave. The best advice I can offer is what others have told me over the years: 'When you're being run out of town, wave to the crowd and make it look like a parade.'"

"Oh, I see." I wondered how I could possibly put on such an act.

"You can go back to your office now," he said, reminding me that he would be on medical leave for the next several weeks. "I'll have Connie in Personnel do all the paperwork and explain the details of your termination, severance, and other issues while I'm away."

"Well, I just want to say I'm so grateful for the opportunity to work here at this foundation," I said, determined to maintain my composure and make a professional exit. "It's been a dream come true for me. I consider myself so very fortunate to have been part of the Foundation's work, and I'm proud of my work here. And I wish you the best as you implement your plans."

"Yes, thank you. I have another appointment now."

~~~

I walked back to my office, passing by Ava who was talking on the telephone, and slumped into my chair, staring in a daze at my piles of work surrounding me.

Then I heard a knock at my door. I looked up and saw Katarina.

"May I come in?" she asked

"Of course you can come in."

She stepped in, closed the door behind her, and then sat in the chair in front of my desk.

"Simon just told me he's letting me go."

"Vivian, I'm so sorry. I tried to point out all your strengths and your strong commitment to our work here, but his decision is final."

"I can't believe it. Just like that. I no longer have a job. What am I going to do? How am I going to make a living and support myself? I'm on my own now, all alone," I said as I crumbled into tears.

"I know this is a hard blow, Vivian. I'm so sorry."

"The worst part is knowing I can no longer work with you. You are the very best, you know. I can't thank you enough for taking me under your wing and teaching me so much about communications work and learning to thrive in this workplace."

"Go ahead and cry," said Katarina, pulling a few tissues from the box I had on my desk.

"No, I'm not going to waste your time falling apart in front of you. I know you're on deadline for various projects. Listen, I'll be okay. I can pull myself together. I have plenty of practice now at bouncing back."

"Yes, but this is hard news to take."

"I need to figure out how to transition away from my workload. Simon wants me to remove myself from all the projects I have going on. But I don't want to create more hardships for you."

"I wish I could do something more for you."

"Katarina, you have done so much for me. Go ahead and go back to your own work. I want to call Ava into my office and tell her what's going on with me. At least her job is safe, since she will be reporting to Janet now. Then I think I'll go home and come back tomorrow to sort things out here in my office."

"Vivian, please take care of yourself."

"Of course, I will. I'll try to remember: This, too, shall pass."

~~~

Here I go again, I lamented. *My world is falling apart yet again.* And I could do nothing about it except pick up the pieces and find a new job.

I considered my job loss a personal rejection; I decided Simon just didn't like me from the very start. He wanted to surround himself with like-minded people—preferably men, I believed—who would bulldoze their way through projects and people and strategies to reach his desired outcomes. He often said, "When the person in charge says 'Jump,' the correct response, without hesitation, is to say, 'How high?'" Yet I respected his position of power and influence. And I knew I didn't have a Machiavellian bone in my body. So I concluded I wasn't a good match for his plans after all. Furthermore, I was too grateful for my positive experiences at the Foundation to allow myself to become bitter about the circumstances of my departure.

It was time to make the necessary adjustments in letting go of my cherished job, coworkers, and work identity. Fortunately, Dr. Barley was on my side, coaching me to acknowledge my full range of feelings and to handle them in healthy ways. Without my job, I felt totally worthless. I had to resist the trap of self-defeated behavior and focus on reinventing myself. *Life is such hard work.*

Everyone who learned about my job loss was empathetic, with lots of talk about "when bad things happen to good people." Christopher was supportive, sharing a few horror stories of his own to show he understood how miserable a job loss can make a person feel.

Victor was not only sympathetic, but also outraged by the harsh manner of my dismissal. He suggested I find a coach to help me navigate the job search maze. He explained Howard had people in his circle of connections who could help me. I was so desperate that I actually contacted the person Howard recommended and negotiated with Simon for the Foundation to pay for a coach. This job coach helped me develop a polished resume, create a narrative to explain my job loss to prospective employers, and reach out to a legion of contacts to gather information that could lead me to potential job opportunities—all this, thanks to Howard.

I had many loose ends—and plenty of time—to begin distancing myself from my workplace family. After the initial "I'm so sorry to hear about your job loss" stage, I found myself being shunned in the workplace. Some people treated me as if I had "job-loss cooties"—as if job loss by association with a fallen comrade was a possibility. Yet I came to the office every day, researched employment opportunities, made telephone calls, wrote letters, and sent my resume to dozens of targeted contacts in the foundation world, as well as conducted follow-up on any networking possibilities. It was a full-time job trying to find my next job.

~~~

In the midst of my job-seeking frenzy, I came home one day to find that Clover had lost a patch of fur around the back of her neck. I immediately called my veterinarian and brought Clover in. The veterinarian didn't seem too concerned but gave me an ointment to spread around the area to help clear up any infection that might be present. I followed these instructions and spent the evening holding her to keep a close watch on her.

The next morning, as I approached her bunny house, I saw she was motionless, lying on her side. As I reached in to touch her, I could tell right away she had died. Could it have been that the ointment worked well for dogs and cats, but was toxic for rabbits if they somehow ingested it while grooming themselves? Did I inadvertently kill my pet rabbit by following the advice of this veterinarian? I felt miserable.

I wrapped Clover in a towel and placed her in an empty shoe box. I drove her remains to the veterinarian's office and arranged for her cremation. I came back home and dismantled the rabbit cage, scrubbing all its nooks and crannies with the strongest antiseptic in the house. I removed all the rabbit care items—her food, hay, salt lick, water bottle, and toys—and threw away the food and packed up the other objects for storage. Now the corner in the kitchen was empty, just air.

With nothing left to do, I sat down and cried. Clover was such a sweet bunny and much too young to die. Rescued from previous owners who didn't want her anymore, she was my final Valentine from Victor. Now she was gone. Forever. I cried, on and off, all day long over the loss of Clover, with Champ licking the salty tears running down my cheeks.

Life is a raging storm. When it rains, it pours these days—never a drizzle, always a downpour. Sometimes it feels as if despair never ends.

Chapter 33

Okay, so things don't always work out, I concluded. Yet I convinced myself to plod along as best I could.

On the job search front, I arranged face-to-face meetings—which I described as "informational interviews"— with people well-connected in the foundation world. I requested candid feedback on my updated resume and explored any job possibilities in their circle of contacts. I took frequent trips to the Foundation Center in New York City to use its many resources for my job search purposes.

I did volunteer work for various associations, including serving on a panel of judges for awards programs. I attended relevant conferences and conventions so I could network. Understanding that it was a long shot to find a comparable job in another grantmaking organization, I widened my job search beyond the foundation world to corporate communications and nonprofit management.

In June, I took the initiative to attend a three-day annual conference in Boston for business communicators from all over the world. With more than 1,000 people attending this event, it was an excellent opportunity for learning more about state-of-the-art practices and networking. Everyone attending would be total strangers, which would give me the chance to connect with other people and present myself as an experienced communications person looking for a new job. So I pumped myself up for being a social butterfly.

The second night featured an icebreaker event at a festive venue with a cocktail hour and live entertainment. As I sidled up to the bar to order a drink, I struck up a conversation with a man with long, dark hair who appeared to be about my age perched on a bar stool. He seemed to be a lone ranger like me.

"Do you see a lot of familiar faces here tonight, or are you a newbie like me in a room full of strangers?" I asked, looking for common ground and hoping for a friendly response.

"This is new territory for me," he said, holding a bottle of Heineken beer in his right hand. "My boss wanted me to come to this conference. And I didn't want to pass up an opportunity to visit Boston."

"Boston does have a lot to offer. So where are you from?"

"California, north of Los Angeles," he said. "By the way, I'm Jay Gallagher."

"Nice to meet you, Jay. My name is Vivian. What sort of exciting work do you do in California?"

"Exciting? Not so much. I do employee communications in the energy industry to pay the bills, but my passion is being a screenwriter."

"A screenwriter? How interesting. Of course, California is the place to be for that, so close to Hollywood and all."

"How about you?" he said with a smile. "Where do you live?"

"I live in New Jersey right now. But I'm on the lookout for a new job, which may involve moving out of New Jersey. Boston is nice, don't you think?"

"I haven't seen too much of it yet. I was tempted to play hooky from some of these workshops but the conference turned out to be quite interesting."

We continued to chat for a while. It felt good to have an intelligent conversation with a man over drinks. I found out Jay had traveled overseas. With some gentle nudging and a few of my probing questions, he told me a few stories.

"You've been to Vietnam as a tourist?" I asked, something I had never considered when all I had ever heard about were war stories in Vietnam.

"Yes, I have friends in the import/export business, and sometimes I tag along when they travel. I like to see things for myself, not rely on what the media tell me about that part of the world."

Jay voiced his reactions to some recent media coverage on global affairs, offering a skeptical view about how events are reported for American consumption. I was embarrassed about not being well-versed in international events. I made a mental note to read more in-depth coverage on world affairs, rather than speed read the headlines, so I wouldn't feel like such a dud.

We listened to the group of mariachi musicians performing in the atrium next to the bar. The loud music interfered with us carrying on a conversation at a normal volume.

"When this is over, I guess we're on our own to find a restaurant for dinner. Have you heard anyone mention a good restaurant near our hotel?" I asked.

"Not really."

"I'm a strict vegetarian so I don't really want to go to a steak house or a seafood restaurant. But I heard about a couple of places from the concierge that sound promising. Any chance you want to pal around with me for dinner, or do you already have plans?"

"Sure. I don't mind hanging out with a vegetarian," said Jay. "In fact, I was thinking about taking a cab to the House of Blues to check out the local talent. Would you like to come along with me?"

"Oh, I would love to hear some blues. That's my kind of music these days."

So we hitched a ride back to the hotel on the bus for conferees, found a place for a casual dinner, and then headed off for the House of Blues in nearby Cambridge. It was a great venue, in a converted historical house with rustic accommodations and superb acoustics. Jay found a table for us, and we ordered a couple of beers as we both became absorbed in the music. Whenever we wanted to say something to one another, we had to lean in close to speak in each other's ear. We stayed for two sets, totally exhilarated by the music. Jay insisted on buying a House of Blues tee shirt on the way out, as a souvenir for me. We hailed a cab back to the conference hotel, arriving shortly before midnight.

"That was outstanding music," I said. "Thank you so much for suggesting we go there. That's something I wouldn't do all by myself."

"It was great. And I'm so wide awake from the music."

"So am I! Listen, Jay, I have this fabulous hotel room. It's a huge suite with a sitting area and huge windows with fantastic views of the city. Would you like to hang out with me for a while? Or do you turn into a pumpkin at midnight?"

"Actually, I have to go to my dinky little room first. I can pick up a couple of beers in the mini-bar and bring them along. As if we really need a nightcap, right?"

"Yeah, I'm buzzed by all the music and the beer. But that doesn't stop me from having a last round."

I gave him my room number, eager to pal around some more with him. We rode the elevator together, stopping on his floor so he could step out. I continued to the 22nd floor and unlocked the door to my suite.

Man, this is really fun, I told myself. *I'm having a blast with Jay.*

Within 15 minutes, I heard a knock on the door, looked through the security peephole to make sure it was him, and then let him in.

"Welcome to my exquisite suite with a view," I said, as Jay walked in with a paper bag that probably contained the beer he said he would bring. "It's party time."

"Wow," he said after taking a sweeping look around the room. "This is impressive."

"Trust me. The first thing I did when I checked in was immediately go back to the front desk to see if I was given the wrong room. I know the hotel was booked solid for the conference. I have a hunch I was given an upgrade at no additional charge because of all the business my employer does with Boston hotels. So really. My employer is paying the same rate as yours is for this room. Pretty cool, huh?"

"Maybe we should pour our beers in a glass, rather than drink from the can, since we're in such a classy joint."

"Good idea. I'll check the bathroom for glasses. Make yourself comfortable on that luxurious couch over there. I'll be right back."

We were getting along just fine. And we were both chatting away about music, our love of good writing, and our careers. My time with Jay was all about friendship, not networking for my job search. I felt comfortable telling him the short version of my recent transition to living alone, including my discovery about Victor's sexual orientation. I also talked about my difficulty in learning to take care of myself and my initial attempts in finding new friends, especially a man who was 100 percent certain about his own sexual orientation. I told him about Nathan, the talented poet who never bothered to tell me he was married during our six months of seeing each other—making it clear that being romantically involved with a married man was totally unacceptable. I made no mention of Christopher, who was the furthest thing from my mind at that beer-fueled moment.

Jay came across as a bit of a hermit, telling me he spends a lot of time alone, but seemed really nice and congenial. He was taking classes on screenwriting and participated in writing groups for screenwriters.

We both were looking forward to seeing Maya Angelou, who was the scheduled keynote speaker the next day at 10:00 a.m.

"These conference organizers really know what they're doing when they put a big name like Maya Angelou at the end of the conference. No one's going to skip out early and miss out on her presentation," I said.

"I think we're in for a real treat tomorrow."

"You bet we are. Have you read her book *I Know Why the Caged Bird Sings*? And what about her poem that she read at the inauguration of President Bill Clinton?

"She's inspiring," said Jay.

"Her poem about being a phenomenal woman is so moving," I said and recited the fourth stanza from her poem. "That poem makes me want to become that kind of woman."

I then had a sudden urge to do something wild. Without giving it much thought, I went ahead and did it.

"Listen, I really love that House of Blues tee shirt you gave me. I can't wait a moment longer. I've got to try it on right now. Is that okay with you?"

"Sure."

I grabbed the tee shirt out of the bag, slipped out of all my clothes right in front of Jay, and pulled the oversized tee shirt over my head.

"I love it!" I said, glancing over at Jay. He looked interested that I had stripped down in front of him without any hesitation.

"Oh, I guess that was a bit bold, huh? I'm usually a pretty modest person. But I just couldn't wait to see what it feels like. What do you think?"

"I think you're pretty amazing, perhaps even phenomenal," he said.

"Really? Amazing enough to kiss?"

"Certainly," said Jay, as he reached over and embraced me with a passionate kiss.

"Well, that feels really good," I said.

"Excuse me," he said, "but I need to use the bathroom."

"Of course," I said as I watched him walk over to the bathroom and close the door.

I waited patiently, basking in the pleasure I wasn't all alone in this spacious suite and that I had managed to meet someone who found me attractive and enjoyable company. *Maybe I'm not a total reject after all,* I mused.

When he returned, I wanted to continue where we had left off. I was tired of feeling lonely. I wanted to feel wanted.

"So, do you want to try out one of these king-size beds here?" I said. "I think it's more relaxing there to stretch out."

"Okay," said Jay rather sheepishly, still fully dressed except he had kicked off his shoes.

I pulled off the bedspread—I never feel comfortable lying on top of hotel bedspreads no matter how upscale the furnishings are—and we climbed onto the bed.

"Listen, it feels good to just lie down together. It's a great bed, don't you think?" I said.

"Yeah."

We chatted a bit more.

"It's okay if you want to close your eyes and give them a rest," I said.

"Vivian, I can't take my eyes off of you. You're really something."

"What a romantic thing to say. I'm just being friendly. I hope you don't think I'm seducing you. I'm not that kind of girl."

"Oh, really? I think you are seducing me. And I kinda like it. I'm not sure if I can measure up to your expectations."

"Well, you're not at all gay, right?"

"Absolutely. I'm not gay."

"That's good enough for me."

We started fondling one another in a tender and curious way.

"Is it okay with you if I take off my precious tee shirt? I don't want it to get wrinkled."

"That's okay with me."

He started making love to me, touching me in all the right places.

"Hey, that's not fair," I said. "It's my turn to enjoy your body. May I take your clothes off now? I promise to be gentle. And if you want me to stop, just say so and I'll stop."

"Okay," he said.

But he never said stop so we kept going.

~~~

We fell asleep in each other's arms. But when the telephone rang with my 6:00 a.m. wake-up call, I answered it and then rolled over.

"Good morning. I guess it's time to wake up and go back to my own room now," said Jay.

"Okay. I need to pack up and check out of my room before the first session today so I can catch my plane later. Do you want to meet up at the keynote session?"

"You bet. I'll get there early and save a seat for you, okay?"

"Please do. It's been a blast being with you."

"And it's been a blast being with you," he said as he kissed me before he scrambled into his clothes and walked out my door to return to his room.

~~~

After Jay made his exit, I scolded myself. Why did I let myself get so carried away? Was I really so desperate for affection and affirmation that I would spend the night with a total stranger, who fortunately happened to be a really nice guy? Or was I just lonely? Or was I turning into a slut?

And what about Christopher? Why in the world had I done something that would hurt him if he ever found out? He was always grilling me, suspicious about my behavior whenever I wasn't with him. I had discovered he had programmed my answering machine, without my knowledge or permission, so he could check my messages remotely. I felt compassion for him that he was so insecure about trusting me or any woman in his life after being burned by his former wife. But I was also angry about him spying on me. Was this my way of getting back at him, giving him something real to confirm his doubts about me?

For the first time ever, I had done something that would crush Christopher. And it violated my self-concept as a loyal and devoted girlfriend. At the very least, I learned I wasn't ready to make a serious commitment. And I couldn't blame Victor for any of it; I was making a mess of my life all by myself.

~~~

As promised, Jay saved a seat for me, really good seats right up front within a few rows of Maya Angelou; she dazzled the crowd with her singing, readings, and words of wisdom. Jay and I kept looking at each other whenever she made a poignant remark. After Maya took her final bow, Jay and I exchanged contact information and wished each other well, with promises to keep in touch.

I took the hotel shuttle to the airport and boarded my flight back home to New Jersey. I pondered the awful truth: I had no regrets about my fun-filled evening with Jay.

Maybe Dr. Barley can help me figure out what all this means, I concluded. It seemed as if my life full of sorrows was turning into a life full of mysteries—a sort of whodunit in which I was the one doing the acts of self-sabotage.

Chapter 34

Over the summer, my life became a series of dead ends. According to my job coach, I was doing all the right things in my job search, but nothing promising had come through yet.

I still wanted Christopher in my life despite his insecurities about me. But all the pressures of living up to his expectations—fitting into his schedule, being a devoted girlfriend in an exclusive relationship, having relentless soul-searching conversations about where we stood with each other—became exhausting. I wasn't anywhere close to making a serious commitment. Yet I didn't want to be foolish enough to let him go—I needed all the friends and caring I could find these days to keep myself together.

Dr. Barley was adamant about encouraging me to move beyond my tendencies to minimize my full range of feelings and avoid confrontations. I needed to tackle my serious lack of self-esteem as a woman. We spent a lot of time unraveling the reams of twisted thinking that had accumulated over the years. I still had a long way to go to develop an appropriate level of self-acceptance and self-respect. My self-confidence was like a lit candle in the wind, likely to be blown out at the slightest hint of more rejection in my life. It took most of my energy to keep going through the motions of everyday life.

Dr. Barley also helped me come up with some ideas about why I behaved as I did with Jay in Boston. On some level, I had something to prove to myself: I was experimenting with my ability to take control of a situation and explore the power of being a woman. I was trying out my wings, hoping to soar to great heights of self-confidence and meaning. I was grasping for a way to connect with someone new, for affirmation and to avoid feeling so alone; I was indeed that desperate for some kind of connection. I had had enough with having to deal with "rejection, rejection, rejection." I wanted to take control of a situation and strut my stuff.

On another level, perhaps I was coming up with a way to hurt Christopher so he would give up on me and our relationship; it would be far easier to let go of someone who was really angry at me than confront the situation and take ownership for expressing my own feelings and fears and dissatisfaction with his stalking and obsessive behavior.

Understanding my feelings and motives made me confident that I could make smarter decisions about how I was going to live my life. I recalled the chilling effect of watching Diane Keaton's performance in the movie *Looking for Mr. Goodbar*, a cautionary tale about a young woman with a respectable job teaching deaf children during the day who seeks the thrills (and encounters the dangers) of trolling the club scene on her own at night. I realized that *Looking for Mr. Goodbar* behavior wasn't part of my core self. I could do better than that.

~~~

Once again, my sister Noelle and I decided to vacation together for a week at the beach in Maine during July. We chose a cozy hotel in Old Orchard Beach as our sanctuary for the week; we worked on our tans the old-fashioned way—lying on blankets in the sand with sunshine beating down on us most of the day. I read a ton of books and took daily rides on my bike, which I had brought from home after figuring out how to rig a bike rack on my Saturn. One day I spent the entire morning writing a long letter to Jay, thanking him for the fond memory of Boston but making it clear I had no expectations other than to be friends. Or was I kidding myself? I enjoyed the thrill of thinking I could blow his mind as a long-distance fantasy. I mailed my letter at the local post office and moved on with the rest of our vacation plans.

When I returned home to New Jersey, I found a letter in my mailbox with a California return address; it turned out to be a "Dear Jane" letter, breaking off any prospects for a love affair. Jay wrote he had a confession to make: He was married. He explained he felt like a real jerk withholding that detail about himself when we were together in Boston. He claimed his wife traveled a lot; she was in the import/export business. He decided to tell me all this in a letter because he didn't want to mislead me into thinking we could become more than friends. So we were both playing with fire.

Duped again, I thought. It serves me right, for being so flippant and fun-loving with a total stranger. I imagined that after I was honest with Christopher about the whole thing he would find the situation rather ironic. Jay wasn't worth the bother to keep him a secret from Christopher—my affection for Jay was over in a split second after learning he was a married man—and I knew sooner or later I would succumb to Christopher's frequent interrogations about my travels and inner thoughts.

Actually, it wasn't long before I told Christopher about Jay during a long, exhausting conversation about honesty and trust. Christopher became livid at first, but then calmed down and thanked me for coming clean with him. He thought it was a good sign we could talk it through and move beyond it. In fact, he invited me to meet his mother in Missouri when he and his boys were planning to have a three-week visit with her later that summer.

"Are you kidding? I tell you I had a one-night fling with another man, who turns out to be married, and you want to introduce me to your mother?"

"Well, you learned a lesson the hard way, right? I talk about you all the time to my mother. I think you would like her. She's up there in years now, and she's not getting any younger."

"Well, let's see. I might be able to come for a couple of days." I knew I could combine the visit with networking in the foundation world there.

"I would really like that," said Christopher.

"Won't she think we're serious about a future together if I show up? I don't want to mislead her."

"Don't worry about that," he said, looking somewhat disappointed. "It's just a visit to meet her."

"Well, I appreciate the invitation. You know, I've read that you can tell a lot about a man by the way he interacts with his mother."

"Really? I'm so lucky to have my mother. I don't like living so far away from her, especially since my father passed away a few years ago. She is a real sweetheart. You'll like her."

"Okay, I'll think about it."

I did work things out so I could meet Christopher's mother, who extended a warm welcome to me. She fed me and chatted with me and listened to me. As promised, she was sweet.

~~~

In early August Victor's mother called me with some bad news: Victor's uncle (who was also his godfather) was in a terrible car accident while on a business trip in Baltimore. He died due to massive injuries. He was only 59 years old, leaving behind a teenage son and his wife, Rosabella. Victor's parents were making plans for a flight from Florida to New Jersey to attend the funeral.

"Would you be able to meet us at the airport?" asked Marion.

"Of course I will," I said, stunned by the news of this family tragedy. "I'll be there to meet you and drive you wherever you want to go."

I decided to attend the funeral, especially when I learned that Victor had no plans to show up with Howard. I didn't know why Victor wasn't going to the funeral. But I wanted to go out of respect for Aunt Rosabella, who welcomed me—a non-Italian, non-Catholic girl from Vermont—into the family with open arms and homemade cheesecake. Yes, it was Aunt Rosabella, Victor's godmother, who had made cheesecake—

enough to feed 50 relatives—at the special engagement party at Victor's parents' home for Victor and me 16 years ago. I wanted to let her and others know by my presence that I cared about this family during their time of loss.

Little did I know I would be the one on public display, without Victor for the first time in their midst.

The funeral home was jam-packed with my soon-to-be-former extended family. Victor's godfather was laid out in the parlor surrounded by dozens of floral arrangements. While standing in line to greet Aunt Rosabella, I gazed at a stunning bouquet, noticing the florist's card listed everyone's first name in Victor's immediate family, including the daughters-in-law and sons-in-law, except mine. *Ouch! That hurt.* But I shrugged it off, reminding myself it could have been an oversight in the flurry of activities.

Based on my experiences with the Locatelli family, I expected all Italian funerals to have lots of drama—and this was no exception. Relatives sometimes didn't speak to one another or were moody or obsessed with gossip. But that day people were weeping, milling about, and talking incessantly before the funeral started. I was aware this was a holy and sacred service with a quintessential Catholic vibe, which already made me feel like an outsider. I was one of the few non-Catholics in their midst, sticking out like a misfit for not making the sign of the cross at every turn and on cue. It was one thing to have worked in family planning, which became a "don't ask, don't tell" issue at extended family gatherings; relatives had made sure to let me know they were intrigued yet disapproving of such work. It was another thing to remain childfree by choice, which was a source of bewilderment for most of these relatives. But, worse yet, I was going through a divorce with Victor; I interpreted their stares as unspoken disapproval of me as someone who failed to be a proper wife for her husband.

I thought I had come to offer support and comfort to others, not for people to give me the cold shoulder. But the

Vivian Fransen

unexpected happened—I found myself grieving my own change of status among this clan.

I later wrote about it, trying to capture the impact of this gathering on me: It gave me some measure of solace to put my thoughts and feelings into words in the form of a poem:

Disconnected

I.
It happened so quickly
no time for goodbyes
Two cars crashed
his head fractured beyond repair

An open casket
so all can see
No resemblance now
features swollen and distorted

Two by two
mourners approach the shrine
Besides me, only a new widow
comes and exits on her own

I alone pause to study the flowers
not the body
Blossoms clipped at their peak
severed ties on display

II.
Gatherers take no heed to acknowledge my grief
plenty of time for goodbyes
Two lives crashed
the marriage fractured

A close-mouthed matter
only rumors remain
No thought of flowers when a divorce happens
no fragrance sweetens that stench

A deceased union
shrouded with silence and shame
Now all connections to this extended family have passed
without any eulogy for a good marriage gone bad

His uncle's funeral lasted 12 minutes
brevity is a blessing
Survivors weep over their loss
the empty room comforts me

Another dead end, another rejection. Although Victor's immediate family continued to be warm and loving toward me, the rest of these relatives—many of whom were witnesses to the wedding vows Victor and I exchanged—were ready to disown me. Victor and I were violating the church's teaching about "what therefore God hath joined together, let no man put asunder." That's just the way it is, from their perspective. No ands, ifs, or buts about it.

I felt the stigma of divorce in a personal way. I also thought about Victor: Would his extended family ever accept him and his new way of life? If not, perhaps it was time for both of us to learn the hard lesson that sometimes letting go, not holding on, is what makes us strong.

Chapter 35

When September came, I became even more vigilant about my job search. I made trips to Minneapolis, Minnesota; Battle Creek, Michigan; Chicago, Illinois; and Washington, DC, to meet with foundation people, as well as attended more workshops and conferences. I started to interview for some real job openings, not only conduct "informational interviews." One foundation, in particular, was close to hiring me, based on the three callback interviews I had that included meeting with that foundation's president and chief financial officer. Then I received a telephone call a few days after Simon had crossed paths with this foundation's leadership. The decision was made not to hire me. I had a dark feeling Simon had said something that discouraged them from hiring me, but I had no way to confirm that was true.

While maintaining my job search, I decided to apply for a job at a mega-bookstore that was opening within a 10-minute drive from my home. Borders Books and Music was coming to town—it was an opportunity to see how a large, empty building can be transformed into a state-of-the-art bookstore. I saw my work at a bookstore as a strategic solution for the upcoming holidays; I could be out with people talking and learning about and breathing books during the evenings and on weekends instead of staying home and feeling sorry for myself during the holiday season. I was hired on the spot when I met with the 20-something-year-old managers for my interview; I made a convincing case that most of the customers who would come into this store would look more like me than the other employees with purple hair and face piercings.

I found a real sense of camaraderie with this diverse crowd of about 45 individuals—all of us were full of energy and high on books. We worked our tails off—wheeling skids of boxes from tractor trailer trucks to the stockroom, unpacking thousands of boxes of books, sorting them, and shelving them in their appropriate sections in alphabetical order by author. We received training on using the store computer to track down book titles and locate inventory, handling special orders, and operating the cash registers. I really enjoyed being part of this start-up crew. I considered it therapeutic work—the act of sorting and shelving and handling brand-new books was satisfying, with the never-ending task of maintaining order among the inventory. I became one with the books—I looked forward to my eight-hour shifts and the sense of purpose I found there. Furthermore, with my 30 percent employee discount, I spent almost all the money I earned at the store on books, bringing them home with me and giving some of them as gifts to others. It was a book lover's paradise in my own community.

Christopher was less than enthusiastic about my work at Borders; it meant less flexibility for spending time with him. But he understood my keen interest in books and my need to do something productive until I could land a job that would pay enough to support myself. And it was easy for him to keep tabs on me; if I wasn't home, I probably was working at Borders.

I also valued my friendship with Kate. We enrolled in an independent film class held at a local university to view and hear lectures about these films. We both adored having Saturn cars and riding around in them—Kate had color-coordinated outfits to go with her purple Saturn.

I continued to make brief appearances at the Foundation's office, almost daily on weekdays when I wasn't working at Borders. I used my office for making telephone calls, doing mailings, and following up on job possibilities. I later received a job offer to work as a director of development at a school and residential treatment center for troubled boys. It was located not too far from my home, and the salary was slightly higher than my foundation job; it provided adequate employee benefits and had no travel requirements.

~~~

My secretary, Ava, and Trudy, a friend from the Foundation's accounting staff, persuaded me to go with them one Saturday to visit the Philadelphia Zoo. We had a good time together, with me driving all three of us girls to Philadelphia. On the way home, Ava suggested we stop at a pet store that had rabbits for sale.

"Okay, but we're just window shopping, right?"

"Of course," said Ava. "I already have plenty of pet rabbits who live in hutches in my backyard, and Trudy has her ferrets. We just want to see what they have."

When we walked through the store, Ava showed me the rabbits. Then she pointed out a small, gray bunny with lop ears—totally irresistible.

"Vivian, do you want to hold this bunny?"

"Oh, I think that's kind of dangerous. I might bond with this sweetie right away."

"Well, think about it. Don't you have room for this cute, little bunny in your life now?"

"I'm not sure how practical that is. What about Champ? And who knows where I'll be and what I'll be doing in the coming year?"

"That's true. But won't it be better if you have a bunny to keep you company while you're going through all these changes?"

"Ava, you're right. Why not? Let's make this the year of 'why not?'s for me."

So I bought this rabbit for $20 with my credit card and brought him home with me. Champ handled this new arrival— I named him Dust Bunny—just fine.

Ava also invited me to share Thanksgiving dinner with her and her family that year; this was way beyond the call of duty, but that's the sort of kind and compassionate woman she was. I knew when I interviewed her for a job at the Foundation that she was a keeper; she not only had impeccable credentials and experience as a top-notch administrative assistant in a prestigious law firm, but she had pet rabbits. When she told me that piece of information about herself, she became my top choice for the job.

~~~

On Friday, December 16, 1994, Victor and I were scheduled to appear at the County Courthouse before a judge regarding our divorce. Victor had invited me to join him an hour earlier for lunch at an upscale restaurant across the street, without his lawyer. My lawyer gave me the option of saving myself some money by not having her present at court; she was confident the divorce proceedings would be straightforward without any drama and told me that she was only a telephone call away if anything unexpected came up.

Victor and I ate lunch together, acknowledging our bittersweet feelings about this momentous day. What a contrast to our wedding day, with its flurry of activity about making sure we looked our very best and taking care of all the last-minute details for our wedding celebration. We had gone through so much together over the years and agreed we were as prepared as we could be to focus on making it through the day.

When Victor's lawyer met us in the waiting area outside the courthouse, he was alarmed to find out I had lost my job. I had a hunch Victor forgot to share that detail with him. His lawyer scrambled a bit, concerned the judge might not be so agreeable to no provisions for alimony. But I had no interest in such financial matters; why would I ever expect Victor to provide financial support to me when I had no intention of providing financial support to him? We had a signed financial agreement; that part was history now.

The judge asked a few questions but the proceedings were over in about 10 minutes; it was a no-fault divorce with no mention of irreconcilable differences due to incompatible sexual orientations of the parties involved. When all was said and done, the judge made his ruling: Our marriage was officially dissolved.

After we made our exit from the courtroom, Victor gave me a kiss on the cheek and a big hug. He handed me an envelope with a card inside.

"Oh, we're supposed to exchange Happy Divorce cards?" I said, oblivious to the possibility divorce etiquette rules may apply.

"No, not at all. It's a thank-you card. And I wrote a letter, which I hope you'll read when you go home."

We went our separate ways.

When I returned home I felt numb. I was relieved that I didn't have to deal with any unexpected drama. But I was also sad. What was I supposed to do next?

I opened the envelope and saw a card with rabbits on the front. I smiled at the image of two animated rabbits facing one another while sitting in a field of clover, making expressive gestures with their flexible paws and ears that looked like antennas. Printed inside the card were these words: "You have the best listening ears."

Victor's four-page letter displayed his all-too-familiar handwriting, in neat print, not cursive style, using black ink. The high-quality stationery was a gift I had given him a few years earlier; it had a masculine design of strong, black vertical lines on chestnut-colored paper. Given the lack of scribbles and crossouts—common markings when he was scratching out the lyrics in his songwriting—I guessed he must have written a draft first and then carefully rewritten the words on this stationery. Obviously, he intended this farewell letter to be a keepsake, something I would hang on to for my personal archives.

Vivian,
…Let me start by saying that I have never loved anyone as much as I loved you. Leaving was the most difficult choice I have ever had to make in my

life. It broke my heart as I know it broke yours. I will never forget the emotions involved nor the consequences that would follow.

Although I have always known that I am not attracted to women the way that other men are, I found in you a true source of beauty and grace. I know that these were the reasons I fell in love with you. We had a great partnership. That's why it always bewildered me when I knew something was missing. It took me a long time to truly put my finger on it, but eventually it became clear that my attraction to other men was part of my makeup that I could no longer deny. I found myself very troubled as to what to do about this. It seemed selfish and foolish to even consider. I knew I had a partnership that few come close to having. Why should I need anything more? I'm not sure I can answer that question except to say it is not my nature to be untrue to myself. I know I would have regretted not pursuing my innermost feelings and that the anguish I felt would only deepen as I grew older...

When I left I had no idea of where this journey would take me. Somehow I thought that despite what I was pursuing, our relationship would always remain the same. I found out I was wrong. I never even considered that the outcome would be an estrangement or, worse yet, a divorce. I still have a difficult time comprehending the true impact. Often, I would prefer not to even think about it. I had a prized gem, and I've lost it. There's nothing left to be said or done about it. I'm truly sorry to you and for myself...

The letter went on talking about how much he loved Howard, noting that it's not only that he finds gay sex to be exciting and fulfilling, but that he needs the emotional support that comes from another man.

He ended the letter with these words:

> Despite how things have evolved, I need you to know that I will always love you. I will never forget the happy times we shared. As you know, I will always be here when you need a friend. I look forward to the day when we can talk about all these things without the intense emotions and see what has happened as a necessary passage. I am confident we will get there. Thank you for all that you have given me.—Victor

Man, oh man, what was I supposed to do with this? I pondered. Was this Victor speaking from the heart as a sort of salve to soothe his guilt-ridden wounds about rejecting me? Or was it some sort of propaganda concocted with the help of Howard to rationalize his actions? At this point, did it really matter?

~~~

Within the next few days, I sorted through my stuff for remnants of Victor. On an impulse, I reached for my wedding gown, carefully stored in a white garment bag still hanging in my closet, and brought it over to my bed. I unzipped the garment bag and noticed how the white lace had yellowed over the past 16 years. I knew I would never wear it again; that fantasy of being able to fit into my wedding gown—lifting the train of the wedding dress into a bustle and draping the veil of lace with a headpiece over my hair as part of a nostalgic journey on my 25th or 50th wedding anniversary celebration with Victor—was dust in the wind.

It was only clutter now. But I couldn't stand the thought of throwing it in the garbage. So I grabbed it, loaded it into my car—along with Champ who loves to take a ride in the car with me—and headed for the nearest Salvation Army clothes donation bin. I drove to the far side of the parking lot in the shopping center to reach the bin. I opened the lid and flung the garment bag over the edge of the red-painted metal container. I heard a swish and then a thud as it landed at the bottom of the bin.

No turning back now, I coached myself, with a triumphant sense of relief. *It's over. We're done. No more strings attached, no more nonsense.*

I climbed back into my Saturn, shut the door, pushed my left foot on the clutch, shifted into first gear, and revved my engine as I sped out of the parking lot with Champ riding shotgun in the front passenger's seat, staring at me with her wide, joyful grin. I rolled down the car windows partway to catch a breeze; feeling the fresh air blowing on my face gave me a sense of contentment. It was a Thelma and Louise moment for us; just like the two women in that movie who escape from their troubled lives, it was time to let go and find freedom from despair.

It is finished, I prayed, as I drove my way back home. *Lord, into thy hands, I commit the spirit of our marriage. May it rest in peace forevermore.*

Epilogue

Ending my marriage was the beginning of the rest of my life. In January 1995 I started my new job with a nonprofit organization that needed my skills, talents, and experience to take its communications initiatives and fundraising efforts to the next level. My new job proved to be challenging and stimulating; it turned out to be one of a series of jobs I had in my career over the next decade.

My relationship with Christopher lasted another year—until he pressured me with an ultimatum: Do we have a future together or not? When I persisted in saying I wasn't ready to make a long-term commitment, he broke up with me. It was a clean break; he told me it was easier for him to pretend I had died than to just be friends. Early one morning, when I was fast asleep, he returned every gift I ever gave him—clothes, cards, photographs, a 10-speed bike—by depositing them at my doorstep. I learned an important lesson: It takes more than great sex to build a long-term relationship. I know I was a big disappointment for him; I hope he found more happiness of his own than what little I had to offer back then.

I continued working part time at Borders, which was where I met an extraordinary man with a passion for both books and music who later became my husband—100 percent heterosexual this time, never married, no children. He inspired me to turn my preoccupation with the blues into an appreciation for opera. He learned to tolerate, and even feel affection for, Champ, and was at my side when Champ passed on after a long and love-filled life. He discovered the joy of rabbits by interacting with Dust Bunny, converting his affection for Persian cats to rabbits—even though in a perfect world he thinks rabbits should learn to purr like cats. We continue to have house rabbits in our lives. He relentlessly treats me like royalty, opening doors for me, taking care of my car, and making me a perfect cup of freshly brewed green tea. He gave me all the time in the world to decide whether or not I would give marriage a second chance. I did, four years later, and we have one of those "deep down, special kind of love" relationships.

I'm told by friends and family that Victor went on to have a life full of adventures, way beyond anything I could ever imagine for him. With strict orders from my therapist to keep Victor out of my life for my own good and self-preservation, I don't keep in touch with him. I'm allowed to have compassion for Victor, but I'm not allowed to let him hurt me anymore. Yet, the world is not big enough to never cross paths with Victor again. For example, he wants to be my friend on Facebook.

As I was finishing my early draft of the last few chapters of this memoir, I received an email from Victor in early 2012, totally out of the blue. He explained he was living in Florida. Furthermore, he told me he's writing a book of his own. He asked me to do a readthrough of his first chapter and book outline; he told me he wanted my feedback because he believes I'm the best writer/editor/proofreader he knows. He devoted a total of four pages in his first draft to our marriage; he has a different point of view, compared to the more than 35 chapters it has taken me to tell the story of the last four years of our 16-year marriage. I won't allow myself to read any more of his memoir; I fear the events of his life without Vivian will rival what I've read in Augusten Burrough's memoir called *Dry*. It would be too disturbing; I prefer to entertain the fantasy that Victor's life became more meaningful and fulfilling once I was out of his life. Denial can be a useful defense mechanism at times, I believe.

And what about my personal faith journey? I have no doubt that God continues to love me and surround me with blessings. The complicated circumstances of my life have not been a series of random coincidences. Only by the grace of God am I still alive; I believe God works through other people in my life, especially through some hard work with a skilled therapist. God has never abandoned me, even when I became desperately disillusioned with the meaning of my life. I still cannot comprehend why God didn't protect me from having to endure the heartbreak of being part of a good marriage that went so very wrong. But I've decided to let the mystery be and carry on with my life. I do the best I can and continue my journey of personal growth.

Do I feel bitter toward Victor and his same-sex yearnings?

Here's how I see the situation: How can I not feel compassion for anyone struggling with sexual orientation issues? I can't imagine anything more personal than coming to terms with one's own sexual identity. Living in denial of one's true self must be sheer hell.

Only Victor knows the evolution of his own journey. I don't have a clue how to play the blame game on this. I'm thinking he had plenty of inner conflict about his true nature for many years, but chose not to share this part of himself with me. I'm also thinking he had difficulty with self-acceptance. We had gay and lesbian friends, so we had exposure to loving same-sex couples and their lifestyles. But Victor never turned to our gay friends for advice and guidance, as far as I know; they seemed as surprised as I was about Victor's same-sex yearnings after he told them why our marriage was over.

All I know for sure is Victor found himself trapped in a marriage that demanded sexual fidelity; over time, as his hunger for something I couldn't provide grew more intense, he decided his quest for self-growth trumped the marriage we had built together.

Looking back, I can say I was able to resist any urge to cast Victor as a villain or demonize his same-gender feelings. I felt hurt, disappointed, and sad that he never told me about that part of himself before we were married; perhaps he knew

I would insist he figure it out before making such an important commitment.

Did I condemn Victor's same-gender feelings? Never.

Did I feel any combination of resentment, betrayal, vengeance, hostility, hatred, and bitterness toward Victor? Not so much.

However, I do have a dream that someday we will all live in a world where people can embrace whatever sexual orientation they are blessed with early on in their lives, unimpeded by any obstacles to explore their true nature. I want to live in a world where all clergy are trained in seminary to embrace the needs of couples who are struggling with unresolved sexual orientation issues by showing Christ-like compassion and offering nonjudgmental, practical guidance. I would love to encourage any clergyperson who performs wedding ceremonies to include some discussion of sexual orientation as part of the premarital counseling process. Simply raising a question such as "Do you have any unresolved questions about your own sexual orientation, and have you talked about this with your partner?" would be a place to start. It may or may not have made a difference when Victor and I met with our pastor as an idealistic, lovestruck couple at 22 years of age. But such a question just might open the door as a conversation starter and serve as a point of reference for further conversations with a caring and competent clergyperson. Furthermore, we would all be better off if we could remove the stigma of divorce—people who experience a good marriage that goes bad deserve our compassion, not our contempt.

Our world has changed in many ways with respect to individuals who are struggling with sexual orientation issues. Since the early 1990s, we all have a greater awareness about the wide diversity of sexual expression and, specifically, the realities of people who find themselves in relationships with mismatched sexual orientations. We can thank *Oprah* and others for taking these issues out of the closet and encouraging people to share their stories. Resources now exist, such as The Straight Spouse Network (website: straightspouse.org), which is "an international organization that provides personal, confidential support and information to heterosexual spouses/partners, current or former, of gay, lesbian, bisexual, or transgender mates and mixed-orientation couples for constructively resolving coming-out problems." Most important, we can take responsibility for our own thoughts and feelings and do the right thing to respect one another.

Although estimates vary—ranging from 3.5 percent to 5 percent—on how many adults in the United States consider themselves to be gay, lesbian, or bisexual, findings from a nationally representative survey based on the responses of 1,197 adults (18 years or older) who self-identify as gay, lesbian, bisexual, or transgender were reported in June 2013 (Source: See the report from The Pew Research Center, http://www.pewsocialtrends.org/2013/06/13/a-survey-of-lgbt-americans/). This study found that the median age when gay adult men first felt they might be something other than heterosexual or straight was 10 years old, the median age when they knew for sure their sexual orientation was gay was 15 years old, and the median age of the first time they told a family member or friend about their gay sexual orientation was 18 years old. For lesbian adult women, the median age was 13, 18, and 21 years old, respectively, and for bisexual adults, the median age was 13, 17, and 20 years old, respectively. Furthermore, a total of 70 respondents (5.8 percent) reported they remain "still not sure" about their sexual orientation/gender identity, and 160 respondents (a whopping 13.4 percent!) reported they "still have not told anyone" about their sexual orientation/gender identity. More research needs to be done to better understand why American adults find themselves in marriages with straight spouses who have no knowledge of their partner's closeted or unresolved sexual orientation before they are married and how complicated life becomes for all involved.

Despite a growing awareness that "it's okay to be gay," some people do not come to terms with their own sexual orientation until after they find themselves fully immersed in a loving heterosexual marriage. No matter how strong the foundation for a solid marriage that allows room to grow as individuals, the marriage evolves into a menacing trap. The torment of daily same-sex yearnings competes with the joy of living with the person one married. Over time, this burden can become unbearable; the marriage vows seem irrelevant. In an ironic twist, revealing this struggle to one's marriage partner is the first step out of this quagmire.

That's how it turned out for my marriage with Victor.

However, most people have little understanding of such circumstances. Developing empathy for the woman whose husband turns out to be gay often takes a back seat to the drama of the husband's journey in resolving his sexual identity. Such women are more likely to be regarded as clueless idiots lacking "gaydar" (a supposedly innate ability to detect someone is gay), victims of a master imposter/scam artist husband, co-conspirator secret keepers, or punch lines of a bad joke. With few exceptions, their experiences are poorly understood because these women remain silent.

I hope and pray that telling my story may help someone. If you or your daughter or your son or someone else you love ever goes through a similar experience as mine, don't give up. There's a way through the muck of unthinkable situations in your life. The only way out is to work through the pain and to find meaning in the process. Perhaps my story can inspire someone else to rise above despair, let go of the past, and move forward.

Acknowledgments

My cup runneth over with gratitude and affection for those who helped me write, "revise, revise, revise," and then prepare this book for publication.

It takes a village to write a well-crafted memoir. So I turned to many people for constructive feedback and advice at different points along the way. Special thanks to Glenn Arnowitz for being my first test reader of an early "memory dump" draft, along with Melanie Rigney for her initial professional evaluation. I am grateful for the ongoing critiques and extraordinary encouragement of all members (and talented writers!) in the Watchung Writers Group and the Cranford Writers Group. I appreciate all the learning experiences gained by participation in various workshops and programs including The Writers Circle, Sharpening the Quill, Women Who Write, and *Creative Nonfiction* classes. I am so blessed to have received classroom instruction by Paula Balzer (author of *Writing & Selling Your Memoir*, Writer's Digest Books; 2011), Jonathan Callard, Waverly Fitzgerald, and Joelle Fraser. I am eternally grateful for advanced one-on-one instruction with Mary Cartledgehayes (author of *Grace: A Memoir,* Crown Publishers; 2003). I also applaud the valuable assistance of Ronit Wagman through New York Book Editors.

I appreciate the encouragement, experience, and expertise of Karen Hodges Miller and her colleagues at Open Door Publications. Karen is a caring and trusted friend who makes book publishing dreams come true!

I salute my public school teachers (especially Mr. Robert Paul!), Sunday school teachers, and college professors who, in their own way, showed me the power of developing a "this little light of mine, I'm gonna let it shine" mindset.

I give thanks for the literary and spiritual insights gained as an enthusiastic fan of the work of Anne Lamott, C.S. Lewis, Frederick Buechner, Jeannette Walls, Meredith Gould, and Dr. Thomas Howard. Likewise, the music of Buller, Balzer, and Aichele; Ellis; George Beverly Shea; Iris DeMent; Jonatha Brooke; Lui Collins; Natalie Cole; Suzy Arnowitz; and Tracy Chapman nourished my spirit as I worked on my memoir. You have all touched my life in meaningful ways!

About the Author

Vivian Fransen is a writer, a thinker, and a human shock absorber. Little did she know when she worked as an intern in a crisis intervention center during her senior year at college that all those skills—defining the problem, ensuring personal safety, providing support, examining alternatives, making plans, and committing to positive action—would come in handy years later when her own marriage was in trouble. Despite her personal struggles, she finds her fine-tuned capacity for empathy, acceptance, and positive regard toward others remains strong.

Vivian's writing experience spans over 30 years working with a wide range of organizations. She has served as a communications officer, a director of development, a hospital grants administrator, a university development officer, a hospice care administrator, a family planning counselor, and a houseparent in a residential treatment center for troubled girls. She has published dozens of feature stories for New Jersey newspapers and magazines. She currently makes a living as a self-employed writer, editor, and proofreader. She earned a master's degree in public administration and a bachelor's degree in sociology.

She shares her passion for memoirs and provides information about relevant resources at her website: straightspousememoir.com. She welcomes opportunities to speak to community groups, marriage counselors and clergy, and human sexuality educators and their students, as well as other readers and book clubs with an interest in memoirs—especially memoirs about marriage and transformation following a disruption. Visit her website today!

CPSIA information can be obtained
at www.ICGtesting.com
Printed in the USA
FFOW05n0248200917